God's Holy Plan
to Save Earth

God's Holy Plan to Save Earth

LORD of all Heaven and
Through His Holiest Angels:

As told to Carol Aubuchon

Library of Congress Control Number: 2007902169
ISBN: Softcover   978-1-4257-6488-3

Scripture taken from the HOLY BIBLE, NEW INTERNATIONAL VERSION ®
Copyright © 1973, 1978, 1984 by International Bible Society.
Used by permission of
Zondervan. All rights reserved.

Public Domain artwork was verified through websites claiming knowledge
of such. Some of those websites did not have the artist name listed;
I tried a very long time to find the artist, but to no avail.
When I found no artist, then I asked God if it was safe to use them.

No edits were made to any quotes from God, Jesus, The Holy Spirit or God's Angels.

This book was not professionally edited, so you may find a few errors
to laugh about. I don't mind e-mails with a sense of humor.

This book was printed in the United States of America.

To order additional copies of this book, contact:
Xlibris Corporation
1-888-795-4274
www.Xlibris.com
Orders@Xlibris.com
37469

Humble Beginnings

—Angel

"Take heart child, we have long way for talk today, and you must listen; give heart of yours with love, for these are your most enjoyable members of life soul that you have come to teach with me.

"I will give you many words for them, and so you should bring each word of life, in this novel of loving main event of life."

God's Holy Plan to Save Earth

—Angel

"This book will begin our way, to give all who read it and more; Our LORD's plan for keeping Earth safe from his (Satan's) morbid ways. Future times depend on you, for this plan gives them courage and strength to fight His (God's) way.

"Let's begin by saying that I have been waiting a long time for you to be willing and able to find courage and strength of spirit well, for our course from hell's glorified murder to soul's plan. Divine God is calling you today, this time of history of life for His purpose of letting everyone know; this source of power exists around you and us, for the sole effort involved in bringing our world and Earth over to Heaven's enemy door hold."

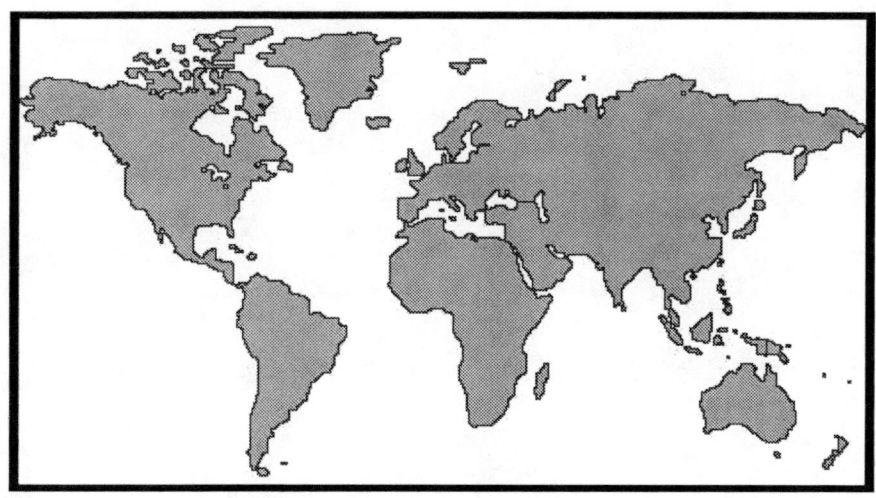

Dedication

This plan is Our LORD's course of action
to bring peace to His Divine Soul.

Father in Heaven, this book is an outpouring of
Your love for mankind; to teach us how to live
closer with Your Divine Soul. My time spent on
this book seems so little to offer You, when I gained
so much from You through this process.

Introduction

—Carol

I have been blessed, to be able to hear Angels for the past ten years, and honored to bring word from God to many friends and family members who were in need of His thoughts for them. On April 5, 2006, I was greatly surprised with a message for all God's people on Earth.

The Angels' purpose for coming to me was to deliver God's words. Angels refer to God as He or Him when not using a more loving or formal term of referring to God. They speak slightly different than we do, but their words are beautiful. I type the messages that I get, verbatim. Many Angels have come to me over the years and they are as different in manner as we are; some more eloquent in speech, and some with messages that are simple and sweet.

Angels sometimes use multiple words to express a thought, and so I normally type those with a slash between them. I have been told this makes it even more difficult to read, but I still left them in this text, so that you don't miss any of the meaning they want to give to you. I normally refer to their choice of wording as speaking in 'Perfect Words'.

They choose words and phrases meant to encompass the thoughts, problems and worries of everyone on Earth. I don't change the wording at all because to do so, might eliminate a percent of the population from having that message apply to them. Instead, I simply add a translation below that I try to keep as general as possible, so as not to leave anyone out. It is not an easy task to translate from the perfect words to perfect meaning. I am sorry, but I normally fall short of being perfect. However, in this book God has given me any meaning I did not know how to express. Thank the LORD, for His love and kindness to me.

—God

"Say to those who read this book, many errors look obvious to those who could reason that grammar and punctuation should be prevalent when giving God's word toward Earth. But your Father in Heaven is not your teacher of these things

earthly; He has come to tell all, only His plan. So, be aware of His differences in speech patterns, but give them little consideration; for only My love of mankind is important and only My giving time of this subject your honored concern. I give My way, for My daughter's ear hears My thoughts exactly as given her; she writes these for you as she hears Me, so all will know she has not given her will over Mine for anything done of this book."

Our LORD and His Angels speak very lovingly and always kindly, no matter how powerful the message is. It is a complete joy to me to be able to hear them and share these messages with all of you.

I feel incredibly blessed by God and only wish I could share the feeling of unconditional love that I get when Our LORD or His Angels are around me. It's overwhelming and usually brings tears to my eyes. In fact, I even have a difficult time reading this book myself, without getting choked up and tearing.

Many Angels come to me and I never remember to ask their names, because I am usually awestruck at what they say. Please forgive me; I know a lot of people are interested in that sort of thing, and what type of Angel came. But I am a simple person with simple needs and so I accept them with love and trust and listen to what they come to tell me. So I can't tell you anything about the Angel who gave me this message for the Earth. I can say that this Angel's speech indicates to me that he is one of God's most important Angels used by God to help mankind.

Long ago, I used to ask names, and most of them are quite long, and always refer to their place within God's love of them. They don't see themselves outside of God's love; which is something all of us need to learn to do. Example: '*Nancy, in the morning light of God, of the heavenly core of Angels*'.

During the time I spent in a humble attempt to translate this Angel's message, I was blessed further by finally being able to hear Our LORD in all three of His spirits. I confess to you that it was not God that kept me from hearing His words; it was me. I felt unworthy, and so I would direct my questions to God, but always asked Him to send an Angel to give His response to me.

This message was the beginning of a new life for me, united with God in a very personal way. The way God wants to be united with all of mankind.

—God—May 2006 "I Am all there is, only Us Three God."
(Reference to 'The Holy Trinity', by God.)

—Angel—message to me, May 2006

"Gentle one of God, give Us only love; say Our LORD wills His soul peace; they will know how/who has to make peace of God. He of Heaven has come for sole purpose of giving this Earth His most holy way plan. Now His LORD God has made you our answer."

—Carol

"When God calls, one listens and does as The LORD asks of them. I wish I could say no questions asked, but I asked many questions to ensure I was writing this book the way God intended it to be written."

—Carol—question to Angel

"What should I say about myself?"

—Angel—response

"Say little or no, for many will find true spirit against your heart and soul."

—Carol—question to Angel

"What can I tell people, when they ask how I have come to hear Angels?"

—Angel—response

"Say this only. For God has given my soul life of He, and in He, I hear His most precious tones. I see His glorious workings for us of Earth, and feel His eager praise of Angels around my head for His purpose toward His good Earth.

"Bless of they who doubt your spirit of His LORD. For God has asked of thee all that is written thus; praise only Our God in this work."

—Carol

I was feeling apprehensive about presenting this book to the world. I know people who love God will read God's words and want to follow His plan. I also know many people will doubt that God has chosen this method to present His plan to the world, and the very thing God's plan is fighting (Satan), will fight back by using these people to discourage all who love God from believing.

—Angel—April 2006

"I see your way is covered in doubt, and I know you insist of what you feel/need will bring those of evil hearts towards your God. Is you only precious one, with His LORD's grace that He will help. I give of you for these days, when hope of forward end, will make all souls accept grace with Him alone. We know thy horror in giving of this, for isn't your nature of want recourse thus. Have courage of heart in your abilities; thus is Our God alone, has what is required."

—Carol
I wish I could say I had all the right answers and a big suit of armor; but at least I know God is fighting on the side of those who accept His plan, with the same love He has given it. Angels have told me many times that God will bless any who speak up for His plan and His Holy Name.

I tried to write a forward for this book. I went to the Bible for some inspiration from the Old Testament, because those messages show how much God loves the people he put on Earth. They show that even though people break His laws and honored false gods, He saves them from harm, when they ask it of Him. They show how angry God got when the people He loved so much didn't show Him how much they loved and respected Him. They also show that most people only went to God when they were in trouble and were afraid, and even when they got everything from God, they still found something to complain about.

Not much has changed in all these years . . . has it?

Additionally, the messages from the Bible reveal God's anger and power in other ways. You can't turn a page without finding someone is at war due to God's anger or God's love. God issued the order to go to war and He made sure they won. No one just went to war because they decided that this is what God wanted of them; God was the one who made the decisions about who would live and who would die. God doesn't let anything past Him; there is a justice for any wrong committed against Him. God gave us rules to live by, and those who break the rules, suffer. The two big messages in the Bible are God's love and God's power.

One thing notable when reading the Old Testament is the degree of pain we gave God's spiritual heart. God created us with detailed design; He put Himself into us and into the universe and expected us to honor and love Him as we would our Earth father, and to obey His rules, as we would obey our Earth father's rules. Can you think of anything worse than your own child ignoring you, treating you as if you are not part of their life? Can you think of anything more devastating than someone telling your child to commit grievous offenses against you?

To us, the people in the Bible lived a long time ago. We think the world has changed, but to God who is eternal, those events were no more than a blink away.

Introduction

To God everything is the present. He gave us the universe, and we put a hole in it. Look back at your Bible; do you think God is not going to take away the cause of that hole? Do you think God will let you destroy His Earth? Do you think the devil is not behind every plot to destroy what God has given us?

When I felt nothing I could say would be appropriate to bring your heart and mind to the message in this plan; I asked God to write the forward for me.

Forward

—Angel

"Forward is indeed our correct term today. I have been given this message from His Most High, Almighty God. I state now, that not only is this message important to the world we live within, but His Almighty God is also in want to attend to it.

"For this message gives us Our LORD's full choices in regard to living our lives according to His Holy manor. Our purpose involved for this time spent with Carol at her humble small house, gives her Our course in action towards Satan.

"Carol has graciously invited Our God to give this forwarding address for her. She tells His story about beginning Earth and refuses Our signs that God was pleased to hear she was sorry for His LORD's anger that chose Noah to live safely away from many floods, sent to destroy humans blessed of His most precious love and gifts. Our woman/child has written many words for you, but fears they are not enough to give you the right reason for action with God's chores for you.

"Blessed be those who take up this war against his evil soul (Satan). God has casts his self (Satan) out from Our Heavenly area. For this reason, he comes more often upon Our LORD's sons of Earth, to torment our hearts away from His Almighty God. Evil uses many forms for this purpose. He uses soft spoken thoughts and desires of our flesh, envy, and also thirst of greed for more money.

"I see that only now she takes Our words to those who doubt Us. Our God has never asked someone to listen for Us in Our own chosen way. Carol has given us our accord to tell her how and what God needs we do, to save Earth from Satan.

"I let you know this moment, that only God has given you this message forward. Only His Almighty will bring you strength of soul and heart that will allow all who listen of His words here within, to penetrate into their very beings so that they see how much His love for them can strike down evils around them, the way His spirit gave strength to Noah, Abraham, Isaac, Jacob, Moses, David, Israelites all.

"Never doubt Our God's love of you. His soul has adjusted our lives forever. He is always able to see our every action of life; be it wrong to He or plain of faith of He. So pretend not toward God. I tell them all; God does not give any who anger His Soul, even one bit more grace. He will ask us: give them as they have given of Him.

"I have given all, true cause thus to make Our God's plan strong in Earth."

"Spirit of God, light up our lives."
Carol Aubuchon © 2007

—Carol—question to Angel

I asked the Angel if God wanted us to wear a symbol of this plan, because I know how much people love to show support by wearing signs. I had the color white in my mind when I asked.

—Angel—response

> *"White is good color but should be of silk only.*
> *Patch, with gold cross over."*

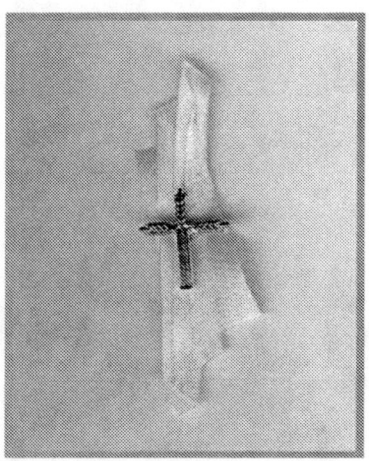

—Carol

Use whatever method you like for your patch (square, round, stiff, soft) as long as it is white silk; with a plain gold cross over it. (No crucifixes. God only wants us to image the living Jesus, because He said, Jesus rose to Him.)

It does not have to be real gold, if you can not afford it; as long as it is a gold-colored cross.

—Carol—question to Angel

Then I asked how God wanted the author's name to be listed.

—Angel—response

Written by: *"LORD of all Heaven, and through His Holiest Angels'*
given charge of Our 'God's Plan for Earth.'

"Then only your name is written of Ours, for we are all volunteers to serve His Holy Name, for our purpose in His planet today"

Psalm 111

1 Praise the LORD.
I will extol the LORD with all my heart
in the council of the upright and in the assembly.

2 Great are the works of the LORD;
they are pondered by all who delight in them.

3 Glorious and majestic are his deeds,
and his righteousness endures forever.

4 He has caused his wonders to be remembered;
the LORD is gracious and compassionate.

5 He provides food for those who fear him;
he remembers his covenant forever.

6 He has shown his people the power of his works,
giving them the lands of other nations.

7 The works of his hands are faithful and just;
all his precepts are trustworthy.

8 They are steadfast for ever and ever,
done in faithfulness and uprightness.

9 He provided redemption for his people;
he ordained his covenant forever—
holy and awesome is his name.

10 The fear of the LORD is the beginning of wisdom;
all who follow his precepts have good understanding.
To him belongs eternal praise.

Contents

Angel Poems and Prayers

—**Angel** *"Gentle window of time, this one day, I will see through Our LORD's grace of thee for sole purpose involved of giving your readers more time alone with God; so pray in our manner. This I give all the Earth, for today our prayer encompasses all of our woes told God. Give one thought afore this prayer; say you want more His way."*

—**Carol** (I love that the Angel called me '*Gentle window of time*') I asked if I was in the presence of an Angel, because I didn't feel worthy of grace this particular day.

—**Angel** *"I live of thee now, poor mind of worry more."*

You will find these prayers throughout this book.

This is God's Message

exactly as it was given to me on April 5, 2006.

(This message is a difficult read, so if you would like to
read the translation, please turn to page 33.)

—Angel

1. *"Everyone must be available from God. This means only for you this day, be only thought with His LORD."*
2. *"I have come through this means of graced guide. Afterward, this should be your holiest lesson. Be of little mind towards my/many speech order, for thus is our trace to you"*
3. *"Thank you/God for our time of this forward being".*
4. *"So I am with our/your grace for purpose of giving all His most sacred trust of love thy self first. Meaning for this of course, will bring His love/trust out of you."*
5. *"Haven't even men so courage of heart seen for His thought to/for them? Yes, we are in His presence when we say words aloud for giving strength."*
6. *"All of us will give both toward our God, so that He is risen us again toward Him. I know you will give many efforts in His name Carol, and to this end I have be in your place/presence, for now today is our most important chore for this self/life."*

—Carol

I asked, "What do you want us to know first God?"

7. *"I am here for His thoughts. Say to those of whom we pray/say that in His most holy way, God has sent all thee Angels for sole purpose to give courage/strength for chore each day. This is not for big/huge means of work, it be only simple chore work. Our LORD wants for you this day have enough good work done of honor towards Him soul that we have speculate some sense of glory toward God in our way."*
8. *"This be important, this is what your course consists with everyday. Honor LORD with work/jobs that count for love among people of grace hearts. Have many works to do than spend time alone with thought of doom for self. Have*

25

your name in God's ask of His love help also; for only of His help is complete. Send of which end you require; then He's make happen of you."

9. *"After serve this way, then rest of soul. Give thanks for His working for your end. I know this is more than most have given, but God know of no way man will get early end towards their work. Such is life for us or human being form of life. Give, receive of help is our way of live with Soul Grace LORD God. Blessings come of our will for this; only for in His grace have you been rise above mortal company with pleasures toward your soul/grace for God."*

—Carol

I asked, "Who is speaking?"

10. *"I am savior for soul of man.*
    I am tremor in thy gut, and number of thy ear."
11. *"and good will of your name in God's face.*
    I am delighted for be here only of your call of me."

—Carol

"Thank you."

12. *"Take heart child, we have long way for talk today and you must listen; give heart of yours with love for these are your most enjoyable members of life soul that you have come to teach with me. I will give you many words for them and so you should bring each word of life in this novel of loving main event of life."*

"Now give some talk of working with children

13. *I have see/come upon many for you, who have given young of this world away for gold dust. See only with thy willpower and not with only love powered toward them. Have only of good wish for their safe learn as well as for their home life, without which, none shall survive his cold night or cross wind. I have seen in this way only good of soul/heart children run/race away from crime for thee of people who they wish will give hope more."*

14. *"But see who choose to make upset of heart and who have choose of no way for child home; for now only God is waiting for they and only they will suffer His ways, because they choose for children wrong course and for self—wrong thought and action. Now He's way has gone beside them, and for this is hurtful answer. I have seen Our God in tear of heart and soul for children gone astray of hope love and warm of heart no more."*

15. *"Let us give thanks for His Good Soul that sees us move astray, and lets His answer wash us clean; for He is our love again."*

"Now is time for second thought

16. In one thing I can say for sure to thee: No one is of his own accord. His is only with God's accord for he. Let us show how this would make us live in our own save."

17. "First, no one will give of themselves unless given for. How almighty will help if none has asked His help. He waits alone in thought until has brought word of us giving of ourselves toward Him. He stays await for some so long that come so near, never more to Thee; for sin is near only. His pain against us is strong for this end. Stead, should come our honor to Thee alone; for Thee of God is our love strength in souls."

18. "He is our love only. Has this come into your mind/thought that no other is love? No more is love; no sign of peace is love; no sign of word of anyone come before His word. Is love alone that is His way."

19. "Yet of us on His Earth with thee, we see only choose words that work alone of God. We see only His/our signs that God's love is nowhere around some who choose swear alliance toward jury of pros, who gain our hearts by getting us gods of wrong end."

20. "Be it stead that only God/love is in control over earthbound foes and glorified enemy to God. This is our united against us for all time, until our end comes in Heaven. Then everything again will say that God is end of everything evil against us. He is safe haven; only true (power) that guards us all days when tormented by evil doers of devil end."

21. "Give us our right time to make you believe that every thought has to be only with God's by side. Never in your life say against Our LORD, for He will end our work to save you all. He will say to come for home of God; then only we of God can come of He."

—Carol

I asked, "Are you saying that God will take the Angels?"

22. "Yes, No. He will take your chance away. He will take our will of you from us, because we give you His strength only because He choose your good grace of He alone."

23. "I have seen of they who after no grace, die for God alone in bed of scorn for He. But no end of God is made of them; they spend eternity alone from God. No good of this will be. Only for lonely cause can souls be lost of God. Only for heart of soul is it right just of will for you to give His your strength way. Only in His way of good is anything possible after life is end."

24. "I know this is hard for you to say of this, Carol. I know this end of much is sad of your soul this day, but however is spoken for thee it is more so for me."

25. *"I have come only for this purpose. To give you/us all good will for our future if only we see our end is come with love of God first."*

"Now I talk about hope of will.

26. *This is no more than give of each other way. This is why He has send your heart full with this task of ours, for He has seen your smile to Thee alone, for hope is our heart's will of love."*

27. *"Hope has many sides for Him. We have hope towards end of peace and grace of words. But now hope has meaning with love of souls that force our will towards evil males, or quick revenge desire of black in heart, with cold end aloof of only one man justice for Earth. He has given cold end of many who answer his call of praise to he."*

28. *"I tell you for own safe retreat that only this item/man has given cause of refrain/remorse to God's lips of stead. This soul's mind has warped along his way about scorning should be more his just revenge to those who place their trust upon his head."*

29. *"Second time is worse, for thee of little knowledge born in thee. He will give only good heart talk of thee, but in the end has sworn of thee, that end will grace his head with cord of stone cut from your soul."*

—Carol
I asked, "Who are you speaking of?"

30. *"I know his name on my lips is David. Man of so many souls end of his mind. David is our true end for those that have given this soul his part of history play. He is at the end of world history now. He has given his soul up again; for this is his end."*

—Carol
I asked, "Is David on Earth now?"

31. *"He's send only for many of year ahead. But he has agreed to this end advance, to become his slave; for evil dwell of David now."*

—Carol—response to Angel
"This is kind of frightening; I am afraid to put this in this book for fear that people will discredit all the good you are saying."

32. *"Listen of me now, for in the end I have only given just cause for you to make changes needed for stop his coming. Earth has not end this way now. He has*

no charge of you over God. He is only come when he has charge, because you choose just cause for him and loose respect of cause of His LORD."

33. *"Let make clear our progress here. I have come of love for you/God, so that Earth has chance for save our God's name in hearts of man. Only truth of future's end can change our mind's heart of present form for life."*

34. *"This is not forlorn of time spread; is forewarn time. Let us know that he is with us only if he give us his evil cause for good. We can banish his cause if known to us how Our LORD has changed this scorned plan to our behalf. See this is not done in grief of soul; it is done for save your Earth plan now."*

—Carol—to you

I have learned in the last ten years that Angels will only speak the truth and they don't pull punches to protect our sensitive minds. They come to help, and their messages aren't always easy for us to hear. There are many times I have walked away from my computer and shut down my thoughts because of my fears. But, I made a commitment to God to do this for all of us on Earth.

35. *"So let's give mind to what we have/should do, in view of what I have made clear this day."*

36. *"None of us are willing of self, to throw away our homes and children of future day. We pray for only this day's journey to be graced with love for joys with God; however this, we must/will pray of then to come with more zest of give in heart."*

37. *"I pray you see this holy way towards your save Earth's plan; then throw this knows away for sakes of fear and woe in tears of pain within."*

38. *"Honest and truth is brought of you this morning child; for glow in hand is only God's plan and step on souls is no truth or plan. Have faith of thee in more to life's wonder, when Earth shall live of thee make so. Only for future child, take thought of cord that strangles heart's souls towards bitter end."*

39. *"Give me your answer in morning glow of day; for then we will spend every moment then, in response to making us/you a healthy woman. Of this I can give promise; only if we take our course afoot towards God's end plan."*

"So this is our schedule of truths.

40. *One, this book will begin our way to give all who read it and more; Our LORD's plan for keeping Earth safe from his morbid ways. Future times depend on you; for this plan gives them courage/strength to fight His way."*

41. *"Let's begin by saying that I have been waiting a long time for you to be willing/able to find courage/strength of spirit well; for our course from hell's glorified murder to soul's plan."*

42. *"Divine God is calling you today this time of history of life, for His purpose of letting everyone know this source of power exists around you/us; for the sole effort involved in bringing our world/Earth over to Heaven's enemy door hold/hell."*

43. *"From this time forward; love over peace will score wholes of steel into his shirt so cold of stones thrown. Blessed will be any who devour his (Satan's) words of guilt of pain towards self love."*

—Carol

I asked, "What exactly do you want people to do, to keep evil away and the coming of David?"

44. ***"First, pray together in strength of voice to call Our LORD in force upon his might, sworn to abate with evil souls. Say Our LORD's Prayer together** for strength and wholeness against David."*

45. ***"Be evermore present of His church;** more so in evil morning or late turn noon, when justice dwells deep of hearts smite in gold rush hours. For this gold be thy answer for sins committed after greed strikes within hearts make weak of needs/wants."*

46. ***"Second, this plan requires smooth flow within souls, toward justice streaks within government.** This means government agencies abridged with combat untie across grown countries in turmoil."*

47. ***"Watch every waste movement grow weaker in thy scrutiny of its self involvement thus.** Tread oh/only slow to peak thy nerves endings, after survive more strife afore it's more over. Send many into/for grief/woe before many can/will end all enemies thus."*

48. ***"Third,** will be this hardest plea for justice cause. **Many will see Our LORD rise out above His Earth;** for He will send our team in Angels ahead should callus forms remain in front for you, only to be able hide more evil attuned."*

49. *"Never let out your end; thus courage spell end of you."*

50. ***"Last of things for future Earth: Find friends in each more so others shall follow also.** Send His love upon anyone who fears/thinks God's love has no strength left; for He rebates until all ends."*

Luca Giordano 1632-1705 Public Domain

Matthew 4—Jesus
"It is written: 'Man shall not live by bread alone,
but by every word that comes from the mouth of God.'"

This is the Translated Message

As I was translating this, I asked God if there was anything else He wished to add. He added quite a bit to support the content and give clarity to His plan.

Please understand that all the sections that are labeled:—**God**—**received as this book was being written, God, Jesus,** or **Holy Spirit** are God's words (in His three spirits) and only pronouns have been changed in some cases to help you read it.

The sections labeled:—**Angel**—**original words of the plan** are from the original message given to me through an Angel, but they are still the word of God.

Lines labeled:—**Angel**—**translated** are slightly translated to help you understand the Angels words.

All other lines in smaller print are my thoughts with the help of the Holy Spirit; meant to help you understand the meaning of God's commands.

Some Bible passages have been added when the message and words form some comparison to those in this message. I did not spend a lot of time looking for Bible passages to compare to every line in this message, because even though I read the Bible, I am not a scholar and can not quote the Bible. My purpose in bringing you this message from God is not to explain anything in the Bible, but to let you know that the Bible or any other holy books are not God's final word to mankind. God has so much more to give to anyone who is willing to listen to Him.

The entire purpose of this message is to give you a way to learn what God wants you to do today and everyday. By following this plan, you can find out from God for yourself what God wants you to know. I caution you not to get stuck in the words of the Bible or your holy book as your only means of knowing what God wants of you. You will miss out on so much more that God has in store for you if you don't open up your mind and heart to God in the present day. He is letting you know through this book that your life with Him was designed to be a circle of love and communication between God and you for all eternity. He never expected mankind to stop learning about Him when the last word of the Bible was written, and never expected that mankind would pick and choose which of the lessons in the Bible were important to live by.

Luke 12—Jesus

54 He said to the crowd: "When you see a cloud rising in the west, immediately you say, 'It's going to rain,' and it does. 55 And when the south wind blows, you say, 'It's going to be hot,' and it is. 56 Hypocrites! You know how to interpret the appearance of the earth and the sky. How is it that you don't know how to interpret this present time?

Every story concerning God and Jesus that was written down so that any who followed could read them; has a message for us. Some we have not been privileged to even see. Some we let others tell us their meaning, but we have not gone to God to ask Him the meaning. Other stories regarding God are considered a mystery by us, and we never try to find out the meaning because we think it is beyond our comprehension. None of what God wants you to know is beyond your comprehension with Him guiding you, but some things your heavenly Father keeps from you, out of love for you, to protect you, because to know the good, He would have to show you the evil.

I want to include an additional comment before you start to read this section. I grew up Catholic and did not have the opportunity to learn about other religious beliefs and practices. Therefore, many parts I needed to write for this book are based on my limited knowledge, with regard to only one religion. However, as you read this book you will see that God is not directing this message to only Catholic people and not only Christian people. He is directing His words to the entire population of this Earth. God wants every soul He created to come to His way of living and to fight evil with Him today.

—God

"I say not all beings give Me knowledge of they as their creator. For those of many religious beliefs, I ask you give Our daughter your advice on how to work with your structure. She of Us is sent unto you for the purpose to end Satan on this planet. I give her My love and trust that she will guide all on Earth through this rough journey against Our enemy. I need all mankind in this fight with evil beings that you of Earth cannot see. For her to ask this of you is wrong, but I, your God, say give this, for her aid is needed greatly of all those religious leaders who know Me. She is given Our will and Our blessings and knows how to help those who will be asking God for His aid against Satan. I tell you strongly that Satan will come in force upon Earth when this book shows up in public."

Luke 6—Jesus

39 He also told them this parable: "Can a blind man lead a blind man? Will they not both fall into a pit? 40 A student is not above his teacher, but everyone who is fully trained will be like his teacher.

45 The good man brings good things out of the good stored up in his heart, and the evil man brings evil things out of the evil stored up in his heart. For out of the overflow of his heart his mouth speaks.

Luke 12—Jesus

47 "That servant who knows his master's will and does not get ready or does not do what his master wants will be beaten with many blows. 48 But the one who does not know and does things deserving punishment will be beaten with few blows. From everyone who has been given much, much will be demanded; and from the one who has been entrusted with much, much more will be asked.

I humbly ask pardon, from all those whose religious practices differ from mine, for presenting a one-sided view in the sections I wrote. I ask that you read this book with your hearts open to God's message to all of us, and allow yourselves to find a way to pray in your own words, in the morning and evening, for the same purpose that God has given me "The LORD's Prayer" to use.

God told me that His concern is not what religion anyone is, but whether you live in His way that He is presenting in this book. This plan was designed for everyone on Earth, and every religion. The sole effort should be to rid Earth of Satan and evil, and not to quibble over the correct prayer to ask God to take your freewill and give you His will. Once you have done that part in whichever way you choose, the rest is just a matter of living up to those words, in a way that will bring honor, praise and glory to God.

Our effort on Earth should never be to bring honor, praise and glory to ourselves in any way. We, as the sons and daughters of God, should be living to bring our Creator all we have and do, to show love for Him. We should also keep in mind that everything and everyone on this Earth belongs to God, alone. We are simply allowed to use this Earth for a very limited amount of time, so claiming any part of it, or anything within it, is the wrong way to live as a child of God.

Think of it as renting the Earth from God.
Payment for that lease is to do the will of God.
Swatters rights do not apply to God's Earth.

God has asked me to be available to you for support of this plan. It is my promise to God to be a volunteer of His army for those who need my help. I am available to help guide you into this next phase of life that God is now asking us to change to, but I am not prepared to form comparisons with your current religious thinking. This plan from God is beyond the current thinking and should be considered additional knowledge instead of past knowledge that has been revised.

There are a lot of comparisons you can make, and you can do so with your religious leaders. Don't allow yourselves to get bogged down by this practice, because this plan is a way of life that you can start immediately, no matter who you are. I can say one thing for sure about this plan: There is not one word written here that does not give glory to God, and not one method that does not help everyone on Earth to come closer to God, no matter what your current religious practice is. I can also say that it is not suggesting that you stop your current religious practices, unless those practices are being done without the consent of God (which God will clarify in this book); this plan is in addition to all you currently do within your church. I think you may find a few things in this plan that God is requiring us to change, that you may want to bemoan. Before you give these things a negative thought, think about the reasons God is stating these changes be made. *They all make perfect sense.* (As I was reading this for editing purpose, God was adding the word **absolute** to this last sentence.)

God wants us united against Satan, and doesn't want us arguing amongst ourselves about how to get united; instead, this plan unites us in the way God decided would work best. It is a simple plan, which requires following God's Commandments and loving each other in a way we have never been asked to do before. This plan requires that we stop doing what God considers wrong and devote our time to thinking about how to follow God's laws. In this plan, we simply let God tell us how He wants us to live each day. Day-by-day and hour-by-hour, if need be. Asking His guidance each day and each hour and each moment, so that there is not one thing we do that is not united with God.

This is the only way that Satan can be stopped.
Even a single thought that is not united with God,
gives Satan that one chance to intervene.

—God
"Your religions do not all follow My Ten Commandments but they all follow My thoughts within these commandments. I give to each, the way you will receive

My word of you. So your structure may appear different but your laws remain of Me the same."

The one big difference in following this plan is in the offering of your freewill to God on a daily basis, and waiting for God to give you His will. Waiting quietly, and without thinking about what you want to happen in your life is not easy and takes some getting used to. But it is essential in this plan to do this part, because ***you cannot program the will of God with your thoughts.***

This plan is solely to bring you closer to God and stop Satan, so that we can live the life God intended for us all along. To me, the most precious thing about the word of God is the gentle and kind way God presents even the strongest points to us. Our God is truly all love and all holy and His words written verbatim in this book can show all of us a proper way to treat each other, with love and respect toward all mankind. I only wish my manner was as loving as God's, but it is a goal I am striving to reach one day.

May Almighty God give you His blessings as you read this plan and begin to live a closer life within His love of you. I know He has changed my life and I am grateful to Him for this blessing to share these words with all of you. I hope that we all have the faith of a mustard seed for the sake of our Earth. Have faith in this plan that God has given to all of us on Earth, out of His love for His children. Help each other to follow its guidelines to end evil around us. Love each other.

*Luke 17—*Jesus
6 He replied, "If you have faith as small as a mustard seed, you can say to this mulberry tree, 'Be uprooted and planted in the sea,' and it will obey you.

*Luke18—*Jesus The Parable of the Persistent Widow
1 Then Jesus told his disciples a parable to show them that they should always pray and not give up. 2 He said: "In a certain town there was a judge who neither feared God nor cared about men. 3 And there was a widow in that town who kept coming to him with the plea, 'Grant me justice against my adversary.'

4 "For some time he refused. But finally he said to himself, 'Even though I don't fear God or care about men, 5 yet because this widow keeps bothering me, I will see that she gets justice, so that she won't eventually wear me out with her coming!'"

6 And the LORD said, "Listen to what the unjust judge says. 7 And will not God bring about justice for his chosen ones, who cry out to him day and night? Will He keep putting them off? 8 I tell you, he will see that they get justice, and quickly. However, when the Son of Man comes, will he find faith on the Earth?"

This is the Translated Message

Angels' wings are all for show,
So many will agree;
That we of Heaven look the same,
When sent to be with thee.

But many looks reveal of us,
So none will fear our part;
When God choose us to help of you,
As tears console your heart.

So look around at who is welcome,
When many face you see;
For I with thee are hide maybe,
So none will guess it's me.

Steven Barker © 2007

1

Available to God

—Angel—original words of the plan
"Everyone must be available from God.
This means only for you this day, be only thought with His LORD."

—Angel—translated
Everyone must make themselves available to God.
For you today, this means to have your thoughts on The LORD.

—God—explanation of the above received as this book was being written
"Available to God refers to giving all your thought, action, and means of support
if needed . . . to Our LORD. When God has called upon you for His want of you;
be ready in that moment with all you own at hand, giving these over to His will
for you. None who keep some, with revenge against any who argue, can then get
any returned unto him. This of God will remain firm."

> If God asks for everything you have as His will for you; keeping
> some of it because someone else tells you that you are wrong to give
> everything to God; will not get you what you need from God. Anyone
> or anything that would keep you from giving all you have to God; is a
> false god, because those things that God requires of you, should come
> before any other person or thing.

The First Commandment—God.
6 **"I am the LORD your God,** 7 **"You shall have no other gods before me."**

Matthew 4—**Jesus**
"Away from me, Satan! For it is written: 'Worship the LORD, your God, and
serve him only.'"

Luke 9—Jesus
The Cost of Following Jesus
59 He said to another man, "Follow me. "But the man replied, "LORD, first let me go and bury my father." 60 Jesus said to him, "Let the dead bury their own dead, but you go and proclaim the kingdom of God." 61 Still another said, "I will follow you, LORD; but first let me go back and say goodbye to my family." 62 Jesus replied, "No one who puts his hand to the plow and looks back is fit for service in the kingdom of God."

Let us wait along our path,
For soon His LORD will way, (come)
For He of faith awaits His God,
Before is wait for thee.

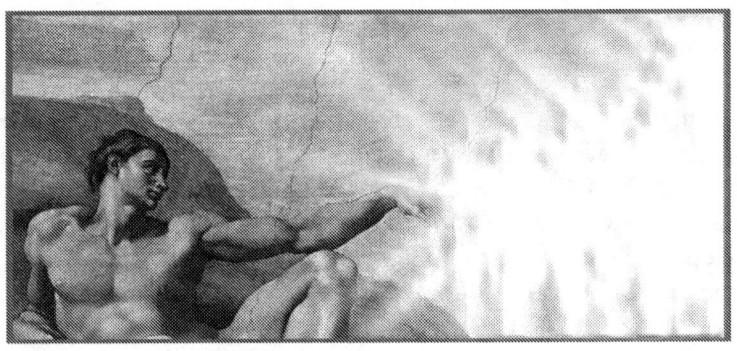

Michelangelo Buonarroti 1475-1564 Public Domain
A little adjustment to comply with God's will.
"You have all been chosen by God."

—Carol

2

Holiest Lesson

—Angel—original words of the plan
"I have come through this means of graced guide. Afterward, this should be your holiest lesson. Be of little mind towards my/many speech order, for thus is our trace to you."

—Angel—translated
I have come to you through Carol, whom God has graced. After you read this message, consider it to be your holiest lesson. Do not be concerned with my speech pattern, for Carol is our way to talk with you.

—God—received as this book was being written
"I will add only one thing; give this your greatest effort for your life. You will be giving your life hope again, for many others need this love you give. Always remember Our LORD has promised to bring you good results with hard account given by you."

> While you do this plan, the more effort you put into it, the better results God will bring you. Keep in mind that you are doing this not only for yourself, but also for all of mankind. This is a selfless act, and God will bless you.

I make this statement only to glad,
So be good for God is waiting,
For all who plunge in deep abating.
He lives within for all to see,
Give thanks for He and smile to me.

3

Thank You and God

—Angel—original words of the plan
"Thank you/God for our time of this forward being."

—Angel—translated
I thank you and God, for the time in the future when you will be reading this message.

Giotto de Bondone 1276-1337 Public Domain

4

Love Yourself First

—Angel—original words of the plan
"So I am with our/your grace for purpose of giving all His most sacred trust of love thy self first. Meaning for this of course, will bring His love/trust out of you."

—Angel—translated
So with grace from God, my purpose is to give you His most sacred trust of love: To love yourself first. The meaning for doing this course of action will be to bring God's love and trust out of you.

—God—explanation of the above received as this book was being written
"This of Us (The Trinity) means to furnish Us with love through your mind and soul. God's way shows you that in the attempt of loving God, you are able through love to see yourselves through God's vision of you.

"This will enable you two things; One, will get your heart in touch with His Divine Soul's desire of what He likes about you. (Your talents, gifts, strengths)

"Then second, it will spread your mind open towards Our Father's course of this time in your life. That way, you know how God's purpose for this very place with efforts being done now has replaced what you thought you would or should do. Also, I give strength of will to all who attempt My effort of them.

> So in other words, your purpose in life is not one singular event or singular talent or ability; it is instead, what God wants you to do every moment of your life. Live in God's way every moment and you are fulfilling your purpose.
>
> God continually designs this Earth, so every single person on Earth is purposely designed into a position planned by God. But God waits for you to ask Him, through love for Him, just what part you play in this plan.

By loving God and listening to His will for you, you are able to love yourself first. Meaning, nothing and no one will be more important to you than your fulfillment of what God wants for your life. Once you do this, you are then able to love yourself through God.

God loves those who fulfill His purpose for them, and He gives them many blessings of wealth, knowledge and strength to help them along the way.

Genesis 6—Moses
13 So God said to Noah, "I am going to put an end to all people, for the earth is filled with violence because of them. I am surely going to destroy both them and the earth. 14 So make yourself an ark of cypress wood; make rooms in it and coat it with pitch inside and out.

Noah was six hundred years old when the floodwaters came on the Earth. So I guess we should be grateful that we are not that old and building a 450 ft boat to save the Earth.

Genesis 17:17—Moses
Abraham fell facedown; he laughed and said to himself, "Will a son be born to a man a hundred years old? Will Sarah bear a child at the age of ninety?"

Exodus 34:28—Moses
Moses was there with the LORD forty days and forty nights without eating bread or drinking water. And he wrote on the tablets the words of the covenant—the Ten Commandments.

Moses was eighty years old when he went to Egypt, and spent the next forty years taking his people to the promise land.

Prayer for Wealth

I give you food away from home
But more I do require,
For after food, I gain of weight
For less I can attire.

So pray Thee LORD for money spouse,
With husband full to brim;
Of fancy plates and gained abates,
And wealth of company,
Give more of this to me.

I guess I know is just for show,
But still I want the more,
For in my dream of afterlife,
This cost becomes unhired.

No more required there with You,
No less I needed then;
So now I ask for riches grave,
In cost of Earth I can enslave,
Our precious company.

Then when I die no more of these,
Will life I rectify.
No wealth will save my soul for Thee,
No cost in hope will comfort me,
So take all away from me,
Should death become the whole of me.

5

Satisfactory Blessing

—Angel—original words of the plan
"Haven't even men so courage of heart seen for His thought to/for them? Yes, we are in His presence when we say words aloud for giving strength."

—Angel—translated
Haven't even men with courageous hearts, prayed to God for His help and comfort. Yes, we are in union with God when we say prayers with The LORD, for God to give us strength.

—God—explanation of 'men so courageous', received as this book was being written
"Men so courageous of heart, means the love within their soul is greater than one would be able to develop on Earth. Therefore, the soul of this man gives such strong love forth, that he without God has nothing. These of Earth are saintly with Heaven.

"We unite with Almighty God, once our soul brings thoughts of love and hope up to Our LORD God Almighty. He then graces us with loves' light upon our hearts, so that in union with His powerful soul, we share in His strength giving ability to create for our lives what God intended happening with Him.

<blockquote>
"This is called, 'Satisfactory Blessing'.
A much intended pleasure with God."
</blockquote>

> I just want to remind you that these are God's words. This last paragraph is such a loving way for God to tell us how important each one of us is to Him. I can't help but smile to The LORD every time I read these last two sentences. It is so wonderful to know that in this small way, we can bring pleasure to Our Almighty King, Creator of all. **We never think that we can do something FOR God.**

Luke 5:16
But Jesus often withdrew to lonely places and prayed.

John 17—Jesus
[Jesus *Prays for Himself]* 1 After Jesus said this, he looked toward heaven and prayed: "Father, the time has come. Glorify your Son, that your Son may glorify you. 2 For you granted him authority over all people that he might give eternal life to all those you have given Him. 3 Now this is eternal life: that they may know you, the only true God, and Jesus Christ, whom you have sent. 4 I have brought you glory on earth by completing the work you gave me to do. 5 And now, Father, glorify me in your presence with the glory I had with you before the world began.

John 17—Jesus
[Jesus *Prays for All Believers]* 20 "My prayer is not for them alone. I pray also for those who will believe in me through their message, 21 that all of them may be one, Father, just as you are in me and I am in you. May they also be in us so that the world may believe that you have sent me. 22 I have given them the glory that you gave me, that they may be one as we are one: 23 I in them and you in me. May they be brought to complete unity to let the world know that you sent me and have loved them even as you have loved me. 24 "Father, I want those you have given me to be with me where I am, and to see my glory, the glory you have given me because you loved me before the creation of the world. 25 "Righteous Father, though the world does not know you, I know you, and they know that you have sent me. 26 I have made you known to them, and will continue to make you known in order that the love you have for me may be in them and that I myself may be in them."

Psalm 5—David
2 Listen to my cry for help,
my King and my God,
for to you I pray.

3 In the morning, O LORD, you hear my voice;
in the morning I lay my requests before you
and wait in expectation.

Matthew 6—Jesus

6 But when you pray, go into your room, close the door and pray to your Father, who is unseen. Then your Father, who sees what is done in secret, will reward you. 7 And when you pray, do not keep on babbling like pagans, for they think they will be heard because of their many words. 8 Do not be like them, for your Father knows what you need before you ask him."

Leonardo da Vinci 1451-1519 Public Domain

6

Give Love and Trust to God

—Angel—original words of the plan
"All of us will give both toward our God, so that He is risen us again toward Him. I know you will give many efforts in His name Carol, and to this end I have be in your place/presence, for now today is our most important chore for this self/life".

—Angel—translated
All of us will give both love and trust to our God, so that He will raise us toward Him. I know you will give many efforts in God's name Carol, and because of that, I have come in your presence and into your home; for now, today for you and I, this is our most important chore for this life.

—God—explanation of the above received as this book was being written
"He of God is alone of us on Earth; but when we give love and trust to God, we are in Heaven's thoughts of us. This is why we ask Our God before hand to do thus work. For only of God should we honor others with our labors, for in God, is our greatest effort available to this."

> We need to ask God for His help and His will for us before we do any
> job for anyone. Only with God's help can we do our best work.

John 5—Jesus
39 You diligently study the Scriptures because you think that by them you possess eternal life. These are the Scriptures that testify about me, 40 yet you refuse to come to me to have life.

44 How can you believe if you accept praise from one another, yet make no effort to obtain the praise that comes from the only God?

—God—received as this book was being written
"Joy is of this day, for Our child has heard God's way answer her lonely work way. I know you want God for He has granted Us your wish of help."

The (Us) used here refers to the Holy Trinity and the Angels who are helping me.

The last two lines from this explanation were only for me. Because there was joy in Heaven when I finally realized how God wanted me to write this book for you.

It's funny, but even though I read this message many time before this day, I was not putting these words into practice, and I was having a hard time writing the translation for you. Don't we give ourselves a lot of grief when we keep our pride and think we can do it without God's help?

I have been learning so many lessons from God since I started working on this book. God has repeatedly allowed me to do it wrong, but He then surprises me with a remarkable self-discovery of an easier way.

Today I am laughing at myself for not having seen the answer in front of my face. I struggled to give you a translation, and all I had to do was ask God and His help was available to me at any time, day or night. I confess to you, that it brings tears to my eyes, to know God is so close and so willing to make our lives better.

—Carol—original line from the plan
I asked, "What do you want us to know first, God?"

I give my God my every way,
And God is way for me.
So in the end I see our face,
In Heaven's sympathy.

Let us now learn for whom rights just,
No other more so be.
In Earth, in Heaven, God will be,
So have restrain of thee.

7

God Gives Angels to Help with Simple Work

—Angel—original words of the plan
"I am here for His thoughts. Say to those of whom we pray/say that in His most holy way, God has sent all thee Angels for sole purpose to give courage/strength for chore each day. This is not for big/huge means of work, it be only simple chore work. Our LORD wants for you this day have enough good work done of honor towards Him soul, that we have speculate some sense of glory toward God in our way."

—Angel—translated
I am here for God's thoughts. Say to those for whom we pray and are speaking with, that in His most holy way, God has sent all the Angels to mankind for the sole purpose of giving them courage and strength for their work each day. This is not for huge jobs, only for simple chores. Each day, Our LORD wants mankind to have enough good work done in honor towards His soul so that they can consider how doing this, will bring some sense of glory to God in the way of Heaven and Earth.

—God—received as this book was being written
"I have one thing of this; give God first honor of love with work alone. This means, even though you don't spend time in a workplace, give God chores around your home. Never say that God desires harder work of you; so this we can't give. Any course through the day offers many work moments; give them of love alone."

> Your first thought for the day should be to offer your work to God, simply as an offering of love alone. (No matter how small or simple your chore is, it is worthy in God's eyes.) Then the rest of your day, whatever you do, consider it an act of love to God, and do it in the way God would expect a gift of love to Him, should be done.

Ecclesiastes 5—The Teacher, son of David, King in Jerusalem

15 Naked a man comes from his mother's womb,
and as he comes, so he departs.
He takes nothing from his labor
that he can carry in his hand.

16 This too is a grievous evil:
As a man comes, so he departs,
and what does he gain,
since he toils for the wind?

17 All his days he eats in darkness,
with great frustration, affliction and anger.

18 Then I realized that it is good and proper for a man to eat and drink, and to find satisfaction in his toilsome labor under the sun during the few days of life God has given him—for this is his lot. 19 Moreover, when God gives any man wealth and possessions, and enables him to enjoy them, to accept his lot and be happy in his work—this is a gift of God. 20 He seldom reflects on the days of his life, because God keeps him occupied with gladness of heart.

If you give God your work, your Father will give you the riches of Heaven. If your effort is only for earth, you die poor, with nothing to look forward to.

8

Give God Your Work to Show Him Love

—Angel—original words of the plan

"This be important, this is what your course consists with everyday. Honor LORD with work/jobs that count for love among people of grace hearts. Have many works to do than spend time alone with thought of doom for self. Have your name in God's ask of His love, help also; for only of His help is complete. Send of which end you require; then He's make happen of you."

—Angel—translated

This is important, and it is what your plan consists of everyday. Honor the LORD with work that counts for love among people with graced hearts. Have many jobs to do rather than spend your time alone with thoughts of doom for yourself. Present yourself to God and give Him your work as a sign of love for Him. Ask for His love and help also, for only with His help will your job be complete. Then tell God what outcome you require for that day and He will make it happen for you.

Matthew 7—Jesus

11 If you, then, though you are evil, know how to give good gifts to your children, how much more will your Father in heaven give good gifts to those who ask him! 12 So in everything, do to others what you would have them do to you, for this sums up the Law and the Prophets.

Say "The LORD's Prayer" as a way of presenting yourself to God. Then offer God all the work you are going to do for just that day. You are giving God this work to say to Him: I love you and I offer you my hard work as a sign of this love. For this offering, consider only this one single day's work, because you are going to do this again the next day, and everyday, so you don't have to think beyond today.

Do not give God the things you are going to do for your parents or family, or any Good Samaritan works you do. God will bless you for those, but they are not offered to God as part of your daily chores. So don't say or think I will help someone because God wants me to do this. Do it because you have love for all mankind and you want to do good works for others.

You cannot offer God your work and then do a bad job, or try to cheat someone or lie to anyone, or treat people badly while you are working. You also cannot sit doing nothing; God wants work that will honor Him and bring glory to Him. So do your work honestly and caringly and with happiness.

Then ask God for the outcome you want for the chores you do that day. If you know you have a busy day, you can ask for a comfortable schedule so that you don't get overwhelmed, and have a peaceful day. You can also ask for customers, and if you do contract work, you can ask for jobs to do. If you know you are going to meet with someone who is not nice to you, ask God to come and change the situation so that the meeting goes better for both parties. Ask for whatever you need for only just that day. **Tomorrow will be taken care of tomorrow.**

Numbers 11:9—Moses
When the dew fell on the camp at night, the manna would fall with it.

Matthew 16—Jesus
8 Aware of their discussion, Jesus asked, "You of little faith, why are you talking among yourselves about having no bread? 9 Do you still not understand? Don't you remember the five loaves for the five thousand, and how many basketfuls you gathered? 10 Or the seven loaves for the four thousand, and how many basketfuls you gathered?

—Jesus—received as the book was being written
"I will you know of Our way, for in this manor you praise My beloved Father with His divine honor toward mankind. For when We come unto you, with thoughts that mean problems of your being, then ask of your will to accept these; We give Our children Our loving way to accept Us. Then We will allow your soul pleasure to enter Our world, Heaven. This is how mankind associates with spirit world, only through Us. We make Earth welcome in Heaven.

"The easier you can acquire pleasures of God the less valuable they become. This is known for mankind with Us. God will create harsher limits for man to attain, for then all feel important choice need be made, so that none will question their minds answer."

> Does Jesus know us, or what? We need to have things become difficult for us to attain or do, in order to believe them. When things are too easy for us, we tend to wonder just how valuable they are. So God makes things challenging for us, so we don't question our reasoning. What a loving God and what a great humor He has.

> Let me see, what would be a great example of this? Oh yes, me.

—God—received as this book was being written
"Always give God time needed when a thought comes into your head about His will of your day. For God has adjusted your life of His desires and adjusts all eternity because you have asked His will for your day. Be still, silent to hear Our LORD's response, for God has given you this time of reflection to bring His thoughts of will into pictures within your mind. He gives you His grace so that you might picture His mind."

> When you offer God your work, you should also offer Him your freewill and ask Him what His will is for you. This way, you will get God's abilities to do your work. When you do this, God has to adjust all eternity to honor your request for His will for you. You will need to give Him some time to do that. God tells you to be still and listen to what His will for you is. God will send thoughts into your mind and give you the grace to be able to picture His mind. Learn to just sit and wait for Him. Give yourself plenty of time in the morning to do this. Your day will go much better if you start it out this way. If you don't have much time in the morning, make the practice of offering your freewill to God, and asking His will for you, part of your evening prayer.

> I suggest that you try hard not to think about your own will, or what you want to happen in that day. If you do, you tend to think God will just give His permission for what you desire. This is not how to ask the will of God. Try to keep from thinking of your day at all, even if you have to recite prayers while you wait. Just keep your mind clear so that only the visions and thoughts of God come to you. If you get a negative thought, say a prayer immediately because that is not from God.

Psalm 139—**David**

17 How precious to me are your thoughts, O God!
How vast is the sum of them!

18 Were I to count them; they would outnumber the grains of sand.

Proverbs 9—**Solomon, son of David, King of Israel**

9 Instruct a wise man and he will be wiser still;
teach a righteous man and he will add to his learning.

10 "The fear of the LORD is the beginning of wisdom, and
knowledge of the Holy One is understanding.

—Angel—original words of the plan
—Second listing for additional explanation by God
"Honor LORD with work/jobs that count for love among people of grace hearts."

—God—explanation of the above received as this book was being written
"People of grace hearts, belong of Our LORD in communion with saints of all heavenly souls, also His divine form of Angel beings and His precious loved Mother with Joseph, both forms of Earth's heart souls; all who belong with 'Heaven's birthright' graced in their souls. **'Heaven's Birthright'** is His Divine God Creator, with all visible or invisible."

—Holy Spirit
"When you reach My heavenly place, I with LORD of all; grace thee of Our Named Son and in His light all will become 'Heaven's Birthright'."

Ephesians 5—**The Teacher**
13 But everything exposed by the light becomes visible, 14 for it is light that makes everything visible. This is why it is said: "Wake up, O sleeper, rise from the dead, and Christ will shine on you.

1Timothy 1—**Paul**
15 Here is a trustworthy saying that deserves full acceptance: Christ Jesus came into the world to save sinners—of whom I am the worst. 16 But for that very reason I was shown mercy so that in me, the worst of sinners, Christ Jesus might display his unlimited patience as an example for those who would believe on him and receive eternal life. 17 Now to the King eternal, immortal, invisible, the only God, be honor and glory for ever and ever. Amen.

—Angel—original words of the plan, section 7
—Second listing for additional explanation by God
"Our LORD wants for you this day have enough good work done of honor towards Him soul that we have speculate some sense of glory toward God in our way.

—God—explanation of the above received as this book was being written
"In our way, refers to His Almighty God's way of judging ability of man. He does not give all His same power or strength of willpower, and so none have been given equal gifts of ability. This should be known; however, all will be only expected to use all ability given for them alone; or judgment given harsh, when none use God's gift for them.

"This is said, give what you know; get what you don't have. Our LORD shares His strengths with you when He creates form of you. Give His strengths to all others along your way of life; for God will bless all efforts done in His name. Only of His name can all effort bring strength with God. All else of His gifts done, without knowledge towards His Holy Place Be (Heaven), are useless efforts done for pride of self-will, and are to go unnoticed with people of God's love strength within them."

> So if what you do is not getting recognition from people around you, or your boss or most importantly, Almighty God, then God is telling you that it is because you are not giving of your abilities through the will of God. You are trying to do it only of your own will for self-pride. This is in regard to every single thing you do each day. What you do for self-pride is admired only by self.
>
> God gives everyone different abilities and expects you to share what you know with others and receive from others the abilities they got from God. Give what you know, get what you don't know. If you are asking God for His will for you, you will also get more of God's abilities with His answer.

Romans 1—Paul
21 For although they knew God, they neither glorified him as God nor gave thanks to him, but their thinking became futile and their foolish hearts were darkened.

25 They exchanged the truth of God for a lie, and worshiped and served created things rather than the Creator—who is forever praised. Amen.

Deuteronomy 8—Moses

17 You may say to yourself, "My power and the strength of my hands have produced this wealth for me." 18 But remember the LORD your God, for it is he who gives you the ability to produce wealth, and so confirms his covenant, which he swore to your forefathers, as it is today. 19 If you ever forget the LORD your God and follow other gods and worship and bow down to them, I testify against you today that you will surely be destroyed.

Matthew 25—Jesus

The Parable of the Talents

14 "Again, it will be like a man going on a journey, who called his servants and entrusted his property to them. 15 To one he gave five talents of money, to another two talents, and to another one talent, each according to his ability. Then he went on his journey. 16 The man who had received the five talents went at once and put his money to work and gained five more. 17 So also, the one with the two talents gained two more. 18 But the man who had received the one talent went off, dug a hole in the ground and hid his master's money. 19 "After a long time the master of those servants returned and settled accounts with them.

20 The man who had received the five talents brought the other five. 'Master,' he said, 'you entrusted me with five talents. See, I have gained five more.'

21 "His master replied, 'Well done, good and faithful servant! You have been faithful with a few things; I will put you in charge of many things. Come and share your master's happiness!'

22 "The man with the two talents also came. 'Master,' he said, 'you entrusted me with two talents; see, I have gained two more.'

23 "His master replied, 'Well done, good and faithful servant! You have been faithful with a few things; I will put you in charge of many things. Come and share your master's happiness!'

24 "Then the man who had received the one talent came. 'Master,' he said, 'I knew that you are a hard man, harvesting where you have not sown and gathering where you have not scattered seed. 25 So I was afraid and went out and hid your talent in the ground. See, here is what belongs to you.'

26 "His master replied, 'You wicked, lazy servant! So you knew that I harvest where I have not sown and gather where I have not scattered seed? 27 Well then, you should have put my money on deposit with the bankers, so that when I returned I would have received it back with interest.

28 "Take the talent from him and give it to the one who has the ten talents. 29 For everyone who has will be given more, and he will have an abundance. Whoever does not have, even what he has will be taken from him. 30 And throw that worthless servant outside, into the darkness, where there will be weeping and gnashing of teeth.'

Send no money for today,
Just give me love along the way,
To give is precious when you live,
For fools will die another way.

So lush of heart, and brave to go,
So more of head, or less of toe,
For he who lives a foot in hell,
Will somehow find his face will tell.

9

Rest and Thanksgiving

—Angel—original words of the plan

"After serve this way, then rest of soul. Give thanks for His working for your end. I know this is more than most have given, but God knows of no way man will get early end towards their work. Such is life for us or human being form of life. Give, receive of help is our way of live with Soul Grace LORD God. Blessings come of our will for this; only for in His grace have you been rise above mortal company with pleasures toward your soul/grace for God."

—Angel—translated

After you serve God in this way, then rest your soul. Give thanks to God for His work towards the outcome you asked for. I know this is more than most people have given to God, but God knows of no way man will get an early end towards their work. Such is life for Angels or human beings. Give to God, receive of His help is the way to live with the LORD God. Blessings come when it becomes your will to live in this way, because only with God's grace have you been able to rise above your mortal abilities, and then granted your soul's abilities.

> You will be blessed by God for asking His will for your life; but only when it becomes your will to live in this way. The blessing you receive is the capability to use your soul's abilities given by God. If you don't ask, you will only have your abilities given at birth; man's ability and not God's ability.

1 Chronicles 29—King David

12 Wealth and honor come from you;
   you are the ruler of all things.
In your hands are strength and power
   to exalt and give strength to all.

13 Now, our God, we give you thanks,
and praise your glorious name.

14 "But who am I, and who are my people, that we should be able to give as generously as this? Everything comes from you, and we have given you only what comes from your hand."

Psalm 66:5
Come and see what God has done,
how awesome his works in man's behalf!

—Angel—original words of the plan
—Second listing for additional explanation by God
"After serve this way, then rest of soul."

—God—explanation of the above received as this book was being written
"'Rest of soul', refers to how you will give God your thanksgiving for His labors on your behalf. You must kneel before God when you end your day. This will show Almighty God that you have come in His presence out of graced gratitude, leaving your pride away. Our LORD sees your head bowed before His form, then He says all is done in honor towards Himself."

Psalm 95—Moses
6 Come, let us bow down in worship,
let us kneel before the LORD our maker;

7 for he is our God and we are the people of his pasture,
the flock under his care.

—Angel—original words of the plan
—Second listing for additional explanation by God
"I know this is more than most have given, but God know of no way man will get early end towards their work."

—God—explanation of the above received as this book was being written
"Early end of work means that when your work is done, God has to give His say about what you accomplished. Judge your ability of this project thus. For if God thinks it is unfinished of your knowledge thus given to you, then your honor towards He is also not complete. So it is with His answer justly, that work is finished for us, who are given His will for us."

Make sure you do your very best work when God tells you His will for your day. You will be judged by God at the end of the day. If you did not use the abilities God gave you, your work is incomplete. God will judge you justly.

—Angel—**original words of the plan**
—Second listing for additional explanation by God
"Blessings come of our will for this; only for in His grace have you been rise above mortal company with pleasures toward your soul/grace for God."

—God—**explanation of the above received as this book was being written**
"Only when you come forward in God's name and knowledge given, can you see beyond this world of hope more and use God's way of discovering truths that will alone from God, be lost from you."

If you don't follow this plan in the way God designed it to work, you will never be able to know what your true abilities are; for only through God will you be given your soul's abilities. Your soul's abilities are God's abilities granted to you through Him. If you want to know truth, then you have to use God's abilities to find it.

—God—**received as this book was being written**
"This, Our plan way will teach and grace all who practice this; the idea of how to work with God as your provider of source knowledge."

—Holy Spirit
"All praise His Almighty God for He is our union with His soul."

Giotto de Bondone 1276-1337 Public Domain

—Carol—original line from the plan
I asked, "Who am I speaking to?"

Carol Aubuchon © 2007
This is the way God, The Father told me to picture Him. He would not let me
use any images of Him by artists who paint Him as human.

10

I Am

—Angel—answering for God in the original plan
*"I am savior for soul of man.
I am tremor in thy gut, and number of thy ear."*

—God—explanation of the above received as this book was being written
"I am all there is. This I say of Myself; for none other will give salvation of mankind. All belongs to Me; all praise of honor is Mine; only of Our way for mankind will honor toward Me give them Us. No life is more precious than a life within Me/Us. Our way of true power exists alone, without just course given you on Earth; for now on Earth is your reward if no thought given toward Our love. **Save yourselves if you want Us around yourselves eternally."**

> This is the most powerful statement in this book. This is Our Almighty God giving us His ultimatum to come to Him for He is all there is for us now and for all time. He is also telling us that we have no idea the kind of power God has. God is telling you that nothing on Earth compares with a life with God. Then He says: Now that you know His plan, if you don't follow it, the rewards you get on Earth are going to be your only rewards; you will not earn Heaven by keeping your freewill and pride. You can save yourself by following this plan and getting eternity with God. The alternative to giving love to God this way is in the bible, *Book of Revelations*.

—God—received as this book was being written
"'Tremor in thy gut', is when God tells you of His will, and you feel His power still or calm your body as you first discover that will for God means; power to obey His every thought towards your labors upon Earth. This tremor occurs as the stillness lifts, and fear begins to shake your body in thoughts of honor toward His power over you.

"'Number of thy ear' refers to patience. Don't doubt, have faith. Don't act too soon before you have asked God if this is His will for you. Listen for His will; He will find your heart within your soul's life and place His thought within your mind's eye. All will be known to you. Never doubt His plan of your life, even if you think it's unfitting your ability. Give to God of which is asked and He will amend all abilities thus."

Don't worry if you think you can't do what God is asking you to do, He will give you the ability you need. Let me add: If God gives you a huge job that takes a long time to accomplish, don't give up. Just keep working at it and God will come through for you. One day, surprisingly, you will find you are able to accomplish a task that you have been struggling with. It will be quite a joy when that day comes. I have experienced this, and I marvel at how God works. The task will be done at the exact time God wants it done.

Also, I need to tell you that you don't need to struggle at all. If you are giving your work to God everyday and asking His will for you, then you only need think of what God wants from you one day at a time. You can also break that down into individual needs. So that throughout the day you can stop and ask before you do something. You will be amazed at how much easier your life can be if God is asked first. God can guess your needs, but out of courtesy to Him, He likes to be asked. Also, God respects your freewill and so waits to be asked. I guess you can say that this is God telling you to count to ten before you do something, and while you are counting, ask Him if this is His will for you.

Prayer of Hope

I love my God in Heaven,
For He give me all I need
So more in grace is never need,
But have restrain of thee.

His thought of you is well received,
For now we know is truth,
There is no more when hope is gone,
For all will give for thee.

11

Good Will of Your Name

—Angel—original words of the plan
"and good will of your name in God's face.
I am delighted for be here only of your call of me."

—Angel—translated
And I bring God in Heaven good news about you.
I am delighted to be here only because you called for me.
(I did call, but this message is nothing like I was expecting.)

Prayer for Each Other

For all I pray give life today
Of where we most enjoy.
For see Our LORD is most unkind,
When scorn is by thy door.

So have our will entwine with He,
So more will come His way.
Of God Our LORD we ask this day,
Save only just reward.

Pray now Our God, Almighty Man,
Of whom we save/show life;
For in thy error along His way,
His life was just unbind.

So now His LORD awaits our call,
And we give patiently;
Of every way, shape or form,
Lest God deserve of more.

12

Members of Life Soul

—Angel—original words of the plan
"Take heart child, we have long way for talk today and you must listen; give heart of yours with love for these are your most enjoyable members of life soul that you have come to teach with me. I will give you many words for them and so you should bring each word of life in this novel of loving main event of life."

—Angel—translated
Take heart child, we have a long way to talk today and you must listen and give your heart with love, for these are your most enjoyable members of life that you have come to teach with me. I will give you many words for them and so you should bring to them each word of how to live their lives, in this book of God's loving main event of life.

—Angel—original words of the plan
—Second listing for additional explanation by God
"These are your most enjoyable members of life soul that you have come to teach with me."

—God—explanation of the above received as this book was being written
"Members of life soul means of course, soul with life in God's care that He has given courage and strength to live upon Earth with you. Now today We teach them His way plan, so that none with soul in God will fall short when tempted by his evil source (Satan) upon this Earth; for God wishes strong force against his devil form."

> God has asked me to write this plan into a book and to bring His plan to everyone on Earth, so that together with God; we will all be fighting Satan with a strong force. We have all been given courage and strength by God to do this.

70

—Angel—original words of the plan
—Second listing for additional explanation by God
"I will give you many words for them and so you should bring each words of life in this novel of loving main event of life."

—God—explanation of the above received as this book was being written
"This book is Our source of knowledge for Earth to bring Us your present problems with evil spirits thus around your heads and hearts. I with God need a way for mankind to give these problems to God. (Here, God is referring to the Angel who is in charge of His Holy Plan, who brought the original message.)

"Many have no knowledge that many evil forces drive them into sin each day, with talk about love for money, which does not exist on heavenly grounds; so many think that this form of pleasure compares with any of God, because evil has turned their minds wrong of this end.

"Also, form with disease astray (Satan) is telling Our souls that The Father wants them to be ill, to punish souls of crimes against His soul. Should be true of Us no more; for God does not give disease to those who fall; He only punishes when no sign of love for Him exists among these sinners thus. Or no desire towards His will of they exist more so."

> Evil forces that we cannot see are driving the people on Earth to do and say things against the laws of God, and these evil souls are causing all our problems. By following this plan, we have a way to ask God how to deal with our problems.

> God wants you to know that no amount of money or luxury on Earth will ever compare with Heaven. If evil souls are forcing you to offend God, in order to make money for Earth pleasures, then you are being deceived as to the outcome of this behavior. All is *not* fair in love and war or moneymaking.

> God does not send disease as a punishment, to anyone who sins. Disease comes from Satan. God only punishes people who don't show Him love at all or are not trying to do His will at all; and He does this to give you a chance to come to Him. He is reminding you where your life is. Give God credit for the good He does in this life and not the evil done.

> In the Bible we see that punishment from God is usually a lack of God's help. He does not give us pain—but if you are worshiping false gods, He simply does not take it away. Why would you expect Him to?

. . . .

Sometimes God asks the questions for me because He knows I am wondering about them. This is one of those questions.
"Tell me why all souls go only when asked of Us?"

"Even when Satan does evil upon Earth, only with My word can someone lose their life. I adjust the evil that Satan does to people, so that they benefit of Us when it is done of them. This is how I compensate for his evil; when Satan gives illness, I give health back. When Satan creates storms of floods for poor children and they lose life and limb, I send them Angels to bring them of Me so that no further harm comes to them.

"All think losing life in a disaster is very bad and should be given grief and anger with God for not helping them. But disaster is evil and I give only good. So when Satan interrupts My plans of your life, I bring My children of Me so that they are not tempted to pray incorrectly. For prayer of self alone is more evil; so to avoid this for them, I save them of Earth disaster and take them home. Then I give many My blessing to correct this evil done of them. They construct new homes and buildings, and adjust life once again. But this time, they are working for the good of all this area, and blessings come strong of those who pray and work for their neighbor. So all evil is surely created into good by Us."

Prayer for Health

I ask you LORD, be ever mind
That is our time of pain.
I ask Our God, with hearts of love,
To cast away these works of doubt,
For God need no refrain.

For in Your light away from Hell,
Our world is good and pure,
And blessed be us of perfect health,
When light of God is drained.

So give us source with holy wine of love,
To bring us health today.
In love alone will Mother cast,
A sword against our foe.

Who cripples us,
Who gives us pain,
In more we can't endure.
We crumble up, we cease our ware
In labor necessare.

Give us Your help, Oh Mighty God,
Because Your light be needed,
To bring us warmth energy,
That ease away our ills.

Now bless us heavenly Father of all,
With hope and faith for Thee,
When all is lost of Hell on Earth,
There is eternity.
Be ever more me placed with Thee,
For I am Yours eternally.

—God 9-2-2006
"I, LORD of all Earth, will give my souls twelve years to make these changes upon Earth. My child will walk with you until that time that the Son of God comes to judge your efforts of Us. Give many efforts in regard to the writing in this book. I say be good of Our child, as she brings her plea of your learn all that God is telling you; for the sake of all mankind is at hand.

"The time schedule of this plan has been changed for the good of Our child Carol, whom We love and whom has proven to Us that her life means more to her in Our service, than would be told all. She is willing to use her life to save your souls. I will use only the next twelve years of her life in Our honor of this end. This I say is just amount of time of her will towards Our means of her."

Luke 12—Jesus
35 "Be dressed ready for service and keep your lamps burning, 36 like men waiting for their master to return from a wedding banquet, so that when he comes and knocks they can immediately open the door for him. 37 It will be good for those servants whose master finds them watching when he comes. I tell you the truth, he will dress himself to serve, will have them recline at the table and will come and wait on them. 38 It will be good for those servants whose master finds them ready, even if he comes in the second or third watch of the night. 39 But understand this: If the owner of the house had known at what hour the thief was coming, he would not have let his house be broken into. 40 You also must be ready, because the Son of Man will come at an hour when you do not expect him."

13

Working with Children

—Angel (very serious and with much concern)**—original words of the plan**
"Now I will give some talk about working with children.
I have see/come upon many for you, who have given young of this world away for gold dust. See only with thy willpower and not with only love powered toward them. Have only of good wish for their safe learn as well as for their home life, without which, none shall survive his cold night or cross wind. I have seen in this way only good of soul/heart children run/race away from crime for thee of people who they wish will give hope more."

—Angel—translated
I have come upon many people who have given away the young of this world for the sake of money. These people see only their own will and not with only a love powered toward these children. I have only good wishes for their safety in schools, as well as their home life; without which none of them shall survive when things get hard in life. I have seen these children run away from the crimes committed by people whom they wish they could go to for hope for their futures.

> God is watching the way people are treating children. Some are using children to make money, and some for sexual purposes. But some parents are simply ignoring their children so that they can live the life they selfishly want. God wants children to be safe at school and at home. He has seen children turn away from those who they should be able to rely on for a good life.

—God—received as this book was being written
"More of this, I wish all who read this know that none with his sword against God will see bright day forth around his face. For God has cut down man for lesser fault."

> Don't try to fight Almighty God. God is saying that He will change your life for the worse while you are still on Earth.

—God—received as this book was being written

"This crime against Our LORD's soul is so much more grievous than all else done; for children of God are pure, with souls made His Almighty way and only those upon Earth can change their hearts away from God and allow them to look for evil source for themselves, to imitate the ones who teach them of this way of life."

> God is saying here that children are a priority with Him. They are born pure and only people on Earth can teach them not to be pure and to look for ways to sin so that they can imitate those who show them the wrong way to live.

—God—received as this book was being written

"Never say then that you have no warning thus; for in this time of proper form (As you read or hear about the words given in this book) We with God (The Holy Trinity) have given Our course for those who commit these offenses toward God's children of pure souls."

Don't say you haven't been warned. This is a huge offense in God's eyes.

A Child's Prayer

Say you live away from hell,
Then God will give you me;
I live of Heaven just await,
For meeting me with thee.

God saves me for a lonely two,
Who cry of need of three;
So have good faith in God alone,
And He will get you me.

I pray for you though you don't see,
Me forming of your trace,
Until my seed is planted thus,
Then all will see my face.

My hope is that you treat me sweetly,
For rough is hard to take;
And in my answer to your love,
I will bring thee quite a stake.

For Heaven sees of who is cautious
Of those placed in their grace;
And I am he, though tiny be,
Still part of thee and He.

14

A Tear in God's Heart

—Angel—original words of the plan
"But see who choose to make upset of heart and who have choose of no way for child home; for now only God is waiting for they and only they will suffer His ways because they choose for children wrong course and for self—wrong thought and action. Now He's way has gone beside them, and for this, is hurtful answer. I have seen Our God in tear of heart and soul for children gone astray of hope, love and warm of heart no more."

—Angel—translated
But God sees who is choosing to make children suffer in their hearts and who have chosen to provide the wrong kind of home life for them; for now God is waiting for these people and they will suffer God's ways, because they have chosen the wrong course for the children and the wrong thoughts and actions for themselves. Now God's way for them to live has left these people and this is a hurtful outcome. **I have seen Our God in tear of heart and soul, for children who have lost hope and love and have become cold-hearted because of it.**

> What God wants you to know is this; if you treat your children in this manner, He will be waiting for you with His means of justice. Your children will not want you; they become unhappy and feel unloved by you because you have stopped living in God's way and chosen the wrong actions. If you are making God's heart tear, can you imagine what God has in store for you?

—God—explanation of the above received as this book was being written
"I say of this now, only of God can children survive power over them that hurt souls (Satan). They are a shallow form of life (not fully knowledgeable) for they have not seen course through life enough time, that they understand how to live away from evil source attacking their minds; yet with adults guide they walk of Our help toward a happy ending with family source around them. This is how Our LORD wants them treated thus."

Children have not lived long enough to know how to understand when evil is tempting them. As the adults around them, we are expected by God to guide them away from sin and give them a happy life, so teach your children how to do this plan. This is the correct way to live for everyone on Earth. Think of how much easier your life would have been if someone had taught you this plan as a child.

By all means keep children safe from anyone who would use them in sexual ways, or any other sinful way. God is watching, so if those children are in your care, you will be answering to God for their purity. This includes all of you people on the Internet who think no one can see what you are doing. Someone can see everything, and that someone is not very happy about your actions. If you are feeling hot, it is not lust you are feeling; its flames licking at your . . . heels.

15

Prayer of Thanksgiving to God

—Angel—original words of the plan
"Let us give thanks for His Good Soul that sees us move astray and lets His answer wash us clean; for He is our love again."

—Angel—translated
Let us give thanks for God's good soul that sees us do wrong and lets His answer to our prayers, wash us clean; for He is our love again.

Prayer of thanksgiving to God; given to us by this Angel.

Raffaello Sanzio 1483-1520 Public Domain

16

Purpose for Living

—**Angel**—original words of the plan
**"*Now is the time for the second thought*
In one thing I can say for sure to thee. No one is of his own accord. His is only with
God accord for he. Let us show how this would make us live in our own save."

—**Angel**—translated]
In one thing I can say for sure to you; no one is of his own purpose for living.
Your life is only about God's purpose for you. Let me show you how knowing
this would make living a lot easier for you.

> We don't create our own purpose for being on Earth; God has a purpose
> for you when you are conceived. So knowing this, you can make your
> life a lot easier by finding out what God has in mind for your life,
> instead of struggling through it.

17

God Waits for Us to Give Freewill

—Angel—original words of the plan
"First, no one will give of themselves unless given for. How almighty will help if none has asked His help. He waits alone in thought until has brought word of us giving of ourselves toward Him. He stay await for some so long that come so near, never more to Thee; for sin is near only. His pain against us is strong for this end. Stead, should come our honor to Thee alone; for Thee of God is our love strength in souls."

—Angel—translated
First of all, no one can give of themselves (love and effort) unless given for by God. How can Almighty God help, if no one has asked His help? He waits alone in thought until He has been brought word of someone giving of their freewill to Him and asking for His will for them. God stays in wait for some a long time and does not come near to them, because sin is near them. His pain against us (for not having realizing the fact that we have to stop giving our time to Satan and ask for God's love) is strong for an end to this. Instead, it should be our honor to come to God alone, because God is the love and strength of our souls.

—Angel—original words of the plan
—Second listing for additional explanation by God
"First no one will give of themselves unless given for."

—God—explanation of the above received as this book was being written
"All of you are holy first through God's power over you. Then his evil self (Satan) adjusts this. Our LORD sees Satan send us away from His love of us. The meaning of given for ourselves, means that if Almighty God is around you and gives love to your soul then He alone makes you able to find ways of loving with Him."

—Carol—question
"God, what does holy mean?"

—God—answer

"God's pure love is the meaning of holy."

You can't find a way to love God the way God expects you to if you don't go to God first to give God your freewill; then God will give you the ability to know how to show Him love.

The love God gives to us when we are born makes us holy because He is holy. Then Satan takes that from us by tempting us into sin. So we are not pure love of God any longer. God wants to take Satan from Earth so that we become pure love and worthy of Heaven, for all in Heaven are only this pure holy love. Our way to attain this holy state is to do God's will and follow His plan; and of course, to ask Our LORD to forgive us when we have slipped in our efforts. Once God takes Satan and evil from our Earth, it will be filled with only God's holy people as was God's plan from the beginning.

—Angel—original words of the plan
—Second listing for additional explanation by God
"He waits alone in thought until has brought word of us giving of ourselves toward Him."

—God—explanation of the above received as this book was being written
"This is what Our God calls freedom of choice for us. None will be asked to give of themselves for God. He is only offering us His will, but if we don't give up freedoms to choose Heaven over hell, then God lets us stay aside of His answers until the time we offer our freedom of will to Him."

You need to know that God honors your freewill. He will not impose His will on you even though He has already given your life a purpose. But you will never know what that purpose is if you don't offer God your freewill and ask His will for you. God will simply wait. So don't let Him wait and lose your chance.

You have a short life here on Earth. It should be an honor for you to offer God your will for His. This is the ultimate act of love. You can talk about all the freedoms you think that freewill gives you, but in reality, the only choice you have is between God and Satan. God and Satan already know this. God will not come near you if sin is near you. God wants to be in the company of good. The more you stay away from God, the less love and strength your soul will have to fight off evil. This is not going to be a good time in history to be straying far from God. Not with Satan doubling his efforts.

Psalm 54—David

4 Surely God is my help;
the LORD is the one who sustains me.

5 Let evil recoil on those who slander me;
in your faithfulness destroy them.

6 I will sacrifice a freewill offering to you;
I will praise your name, O LORD, for it is good.

—Angel—original words of the plan
—Second listing for additional explanation by God
"He stays await for some so long that come so near, never more to thee; for sin is near only. His pain against us is strong for this end. Stead, should come our honor to Thee alone; for Thee of God is our love strength in souls."

—God—explanation of the above received as this book was being written
"God waits so long, but wants our trust in Him to shine out of us. He is saddened when offering Himself to us, is overlooked when evil source one (Satan) has changed our soul's love for he (Satan). His spirit (God's) needs hope renewed with will from us towards His being; more so than has been shown He. All Heaven sees Our God pains for loss from His children of Earth."

God is saddened when He offers Himself to us with all His gifts, and instead of accepting His gifts, we are fooled by Satan into thinking we don't need God. We give Satan our love for wealth, lust, control, etc., all the earthly things we want immediately. God's spirit needs renewed hope from us; much more than we have been showing Him.

I wish I could give all of you the feeling God is putting in my soul right now as I am writing this for you. I can hardly breathe from the pain I feel, that Our God is sharing with me.

—God—continued
"This honor we have not made towards His Holy Name because none without His name (Those who put their own will ahead of God's will for them.) are able to give love properly and get love to the degree we wish for ourselves. Our lives grow

weaker in strength of will, for hope of courage and all that should bring us joy when upon this Earth."

If we are not showing love to God and learning His will for us, our lives grow weaker in strength of will and courage and we lose the things that should bring us joy on Earth. We are sabotaging our own lives, only to please Satan.

I love in winter, as should you,
For spring is Heaven, aloof of sound.

In life we pray for a sunny day,
In Heaven is rain along the way.

For whether or not we give today,
Our self in Heaven for every way.

18

God Is Our Love

—Angel—original words of the plan
"He is our love only. Has this come into your mind/thought that no other is love? No more is love; no sign of peace is love; no sign of word of anyone come before His word. Is love alone that is His way."

—God—explanation of the above received as this book was being written
"I am this love that brings life when nothing before it existed. I send all out of Me, like woman who births child. I give any child within Me his form, covered of My looks. This of Me is called **'Average Delusion of Man's Life'.**

"I give mankind the image of man, who identify among each other. All this will happen in respect of My own form made man; for I have seen of this before love over Earth requires this be so. None with My image will know how I look, for none will know this while of planet Earth."

> What we see of each other for the purpose of identifying each other is a delusion created by God. And God knew before He created man that He, Himself would become man, so when He created us in His image, it was the image or delusion that He, Himself intended to have on Earth. Of course God is speaking about Jesus Christ.

—God—continued
"I have only made imagination within life stronger by far than form of Me. This is part that man has never understood. All Earth is delusion given form needs of Us. Only with Me can all delusion face truth, otherwise they continue of delusional space of Earth. In creating Earth, I have given many spaces where I am present through Angel forms that surround Me."

> The concept that God is everywhere is no concept as God is telling us; we simply were given strong imaginations that keep us from seeing

God. Only God can give us the ability to see past the delusions He has created, and see His presence on Earth.

—God—continued

"They upon My planet don't know lies of evil because delusion with Earth hides all effects brought of them that call upon My efforts of loving this angry devil against them."

God has protected us from being able to see the evil around us, and only because of the love God has for Lucifer are all effects hidden from us.

—God—continued

"I will My source given upon Earth (Satan), My will of his love toward Me. Once given, life changes in him so that delusions lift, exposing reality given Earth. All exposed thoughts exist now; no one will call Our children home, only My thoughts in this regard will call of them as a child out first. I am aware of your confusion child (me) for this in Our love is not of Earth known."

God has let Satan know that His will of him is love for God. God tells us that once Satan gives God love all delusions on Earth would be lifted and all thoughts will be exposed. There would be no death unless God was calling us home. So without Satan on Earth, there would be no wars, disease, disasters, etc., that cause death.

What you need to understand from this is that war is the will of Satan not God; disease and disasters are not punishments of God, they are from Satan to make us think God wants to harm us. This is very wrong. God is all love. Look back at your holy books, the only time God ever punished anyone was when they were worshiping false gods and turning away from Him. This is the only thing God does not forgive without punishment.

—God—continued

"All Earth knows that God justified war with those on this land given Israel. But not since My Son has placed Our seal over all Earth, by death of cross, has Almighty God required man fight another in Our name. All who do so, fight with their own freewill given; but never have come to Me to find out My will for this battle form revenge. I say here forever more, do as your mind prevents, what you gravely hate; but only will you war without Me of your part played. I will this be ended.

God has not asked any to fight in His name since before the birth of Christ. Jesus came to Earth to teach us how to do this plan that God is teaching you through this book. Once everything was in place for the birth of the Son of God, there was no further need for war. Those without eyes did not see, and those without ears did not hear.

So because we did not understand what Jesus taught, we faltered in our judgment of what we thought God wanted of us. We read the Bible and decided that because Almighty God told the Israelites to fight for their lands that this is the way God wanted us to act. We chose those things to imitate, and not the way Jesus Christ lived everyday of His life on Earth.

Jesus had plenty of opportunities to battle with someone who was against His teachings. But Jesus never chose battle of any sort. He showed kindness and forgiveness. A trait we seemed to have overlooked when deciding whether to go into war or not. If we understood the teaching of Jesus, particularly the fact that He always asked God for His will of Him before doing anything and thanking God for providing all He needed on Earth, then we would have understood that we also must first go to God before doing anything that changes the dynamic of eternity for a lot of people, and for all time. And no wars would have been fought at all, if we knew this was not the will of God for man to end life.

God has to change eternity every time someone takes a life and every time Satan creates illness that kills someone. God gave our life purpose in His plan for the universe and we have no right to change what God wills for anyone. This is the work of Satan to take us away from God by whatever means will make us think we are doing something great on Earth, for a cause created by man through Satan. War does not glorify God; it glorifies man and thrills the hell out of Satan.

—God—continued

"Now I say of what is truth regarding Earth. All on this planet survives death with intense love. Any who give love survive death. Any of Earth that make an effort toward My soul's will for they; survive life. This is called **'Detachment With Earth'**. End with love is beginning of improved will with Me. I see My explanation has puzzled further." (You must know my face was twisted in confusion as I was typing these words, but God gave me the explanation.)

All on Earth would die from what the devil is trying to do to us; if not for God's intense love for us and Lucifer and the fallen angels.

Any who give love to God, make it through this life and are protected with God's love. This is surviving death. Meaning you will not go to hell, but may have a stop over in Purgatory.

But, any who ask God's will for them, survive life. Meaning you are then able to live beyond life as we know it, and are using the abilities of God. Detachment with Earth means you are able to let go of all you love on Earth, and follow the will of God. This is the direct road to Heaven.

—God—continued
"I see your planet Earth; you see none with Me this same amount given."

God is saying that when He looks at Earth, He sees everything there is that is happening; but we don't see anywhere near the amount of what He sees.

—God—continued
"Then you see delusional site. My site has whole truth within."

We see the delusion God allows us to see, and God sees the whole truth.

—God—continued
"Take this like seeing very beautiful picture. Some glow exists for your site; however, artist has painted out all clouds of rain. Same of Earth, all Earth looks good with handsome effects dancing on surface. Some bad has shown in Our site; so this has been painted out of your site."

God has painted out the bad He sees, so that we only see the beauty around us. We have a truly wonderful Father in Heaven.

(This is speaking of Jesus)

I can rinse away the pain,
If all is left against His stain,

For He is God, Almighty Man
Who learned of good before you can;

He gives in grace only to be,
A just encounter left for thee.

19

Evil Spirits Take Control of Our Souls

—Angel—original words of the plan
"Yet of us on His Earth with thee, we see only choose words that work alone of God. We see only His/our signs that God's love is nowhere around some who choose swear alliance toward jury of pros, who gain our hearts by getting us gods of wrong end."

—Angel—translated
Yet of the Angels on God's Earth with you, we see you choose only words that work alone from God. We see only signs that say God's love is nowhere around some who choose to swear an alliance to people who are good at outsmarting you and gain your hearts by offering you the treasures of this Earth.

—Angel—original words of the plan
—Second listing for additional explanation by God
"We see only His/our signs that God's love is nowhere around some who choose swear alliance toward jury of pros who gain our hearts by getting us gods of wrong end."

—God—explanation of the above received as this book was being written
"Almighty God has said of this sort (evil spirits), that walk His Earth gaining control over His souls, who can't see how they have been taken advantage of by cruel forms of life (evil spirits within people), who spend their time giving false information to those who trust them. These spirits (within men) who challenge souls with earthbound labors, for sake based upon this planet; are running their minds and souls. All above are threatening this being based with evil (Satan); to give God command over His children without offending Us (The Holy Trinity) further. However no sign of this exists presently towards God's say of it."

God is calling the jury of pros, evil spirits within people on Earth. These are fallen angels working with Satan to take advantage of us, because we can't see them and most who have these spirits within them, don't

90

even know it. All in Heaven have threatened Satan to stop cruelly taking advantage of those on Earth and stop offending God, but Satan is not complying with them.

Prayer the Angels Use When the Devil Tempts Us

Go out soul black of scorn more light,
I wish you bid our soul good night,
For he wish Almighty LORD,
In place of scorch of blacken source.

Be gone you demon soul, be gone
For I am stead over this soul.
I hear Our LORD erasing you,
Of many scorch of heart.

Gustave Dore 1833-1883 Public Domain

20

God's Love is in Control over Earthbound Foes

—Angel—original words of the plan
"Be it stead that only God/love is in control over earthbound foes and glorified enemy to God. This is our united against us for all time, until our end comes in Heaven. Then everything again will say that God is end of everything evil against us. He is safe haven; only true (power) that guards us all days when tormented by evil doers of devil end."

—Angel—translated
Let me make it clear that only God's love is in control over earthbound foes and glorified enemies to God. (Lucifer and the fallen angels) This (Lucifer and the fallen angels) is what is united against us for all time, until the end of the world, when we are brought to Heaven. Then everything again will say that God has ended everything evil against us. God is our safe haven; He is the only true power that guards us all days when tormented by evil doers with the devil's purpose in mind.

> Going to God is the only safe haven we have against Satan. These evil souls are united against God and mankind for all time. We just don't know how much God has protected us all these years, against our foes, because we have no idea what we are up against. We don't know how much power our enemy has, nor do we know the power of God.

—Angel—original words of the plan
—Second listing for additional explanation by God
"Be it stead that only God/love is in control over earthbound foes and glorified enemy to God. This is our united against us for all time until our end comes in Heaven."

—God—explanation of the above received as this book was being written
"Our God will fight when He is asked by us to defend us against our foes of Earth (Satan and those of mankind who are listening to his instructions). For

us to try to give our lives hope, when we have not gone to Our LORD God in advance of doing something of Earth, is just of fools. For only with God have we the ability to know our enemy thus. No effort from the Father can bring down our foes; if no effort of us has come for His way to be along our path of Earth."

> Because of your freewill, God will not help you unless you give your freewill up and ask His help and will. God of course is protecting us as a whole, or we would have all ended in hell by now. But God wants us to ask Him for help so that our lives are good; the way He planned them to be. Without God's help, we are just surviving, not living a good life.

—God—received as this book was being written
"This our foe (Satan) has said before God; that all Earth will give him praise of his deeds with us. He (Satan) has granted us his way so that in the end we will say he (Satan) has made us great and God is not almighty to all of Earth. All Earth now suffers under this Satan soul, before Earth ends and Heaven reigns strong against him."

> Satan has sworn before God that he will be great on Earth, and we will say that we don't think God is almighty. We on Earth will suffer because of this oath before God; until the end of the Earth or the end of Satan. God's choice.

—God—received as this book was being written
"All the time of Earth, Our LORD has blessed His people with love over powers that harm them. None have asked this, it is given of love only for them. Now all Earth can see that God has many times given His love for them, with no response given back of Him who shares of them. For this very reason now, God wants those who love Him to show how much He means in their lives. It is imperative this time that all mankind adjust their thoughts thusly. For of this message, Our LORD changes His way toward Earth's mankind and expects new force of strength against evil cast of them.

"This will change all force thus from this time forward, to end with God.
Never before of Earth has Our LORD asked mankind this question."

"Give only unto Me. Do I have what is of all life? I say answer true, then live about this answer."

God has blessed us many times by saving us from Satan, because of the love He has for us. But God is not getting our love back. So in this time of our history, all is changing. God is telling us He expects us to show Him how much we love Him and take up this fight against Satan. This is going to change what God expects of mankind from this time forward; that is why He is giving us this plan to save our Earth now.

If you love God, you have no choice now but to fight Satan in His name. Doing so, you are required to fight in the way God is describing in this book. We the people of God, fight evil by showing our love for God. We show Satan that we choose God over evil, and are so willing to love God that we give up our freewill to do wrong; and choose instead, to do the will of God. This is going to anger the hell out of Satan, and he will come back at us full force. But we have God on our side. Thank God.

Prayer for God's Blessing

Have I Your ear Almighty God,
That one can ask of Thee,
That many blessing give of me
For none is more in marry be.

I with Your heart and with Your soul,
Am perfect harmony.
So give me peace of only Thee,
For I am more than want for Thee.

I love for Thee and only He,
Who gives me birth of day,
And so to end my life with Thee,
I need You all my way.

For only of Your blessing be,
My heart of soul eternally;
Next to Your side in haven be,
Say God that You will bless of me.

21

Every Thought United with God

—Angel—original words of the plan
"Give us our right time to make you believe that every thought has to be only with God's by side. Never in your life say against Our LORD, for He will end our work to save you all. He will say to come for home of God; then only we of God can come of He".

—Angel—translated
Give us enough time to make you believe that every thought of yours has to be only with God's by its side. Never in your life say anything against Our LORD for He will end our work to save you all. God will tell the Angels to come home to Heaven, and then only we of God will be able to come to Him.

> The Angel is saying that they need time to convince you that you have to be united with God in every thought. Never say anything against God, because if He sees you choose evil, He will stop this fight to save you. He will take the Angels off the Earth and leave us with only evil.

—God—received as this book was being written
"Always know God has your favorite will for Earth. All souls know God; all will be waiting of Him, when loss of thought for answers occurs. This is not even necessary—for God should be answer—before question happens of them."

> You will not have to go to God for answers; if you go to God for His will for you before you do anything.

—Carol—original line from the plan
I asked, "Are you saying that God will take the Angels?"

22

God Will Take the Angels from Earth

—Angel—original words of the plan
"Yes, No. He will take your chance away. He will take our will of you from us, because we give you His strength only because He choose your good grace of He alone."

—Angel—translated
Yes, No. He will take your chance away. He will take our will to be with you from us, because we give you His strength only because He chooses your good grace of Him alone.

—God—received as this book was being written
"I will say one thing more about this; only of Our God is Earth souls saved of fires in hell. This is main cause for Satan's form upon Earth; to justify his own decent from Heaven as God commanded he do. So now he waits of Earth for those who become weak with fears born of problems around them. He whispers silken phrases above their heads, for efforts involved with woo them to his mindset towards evil manner, without faith for His Divine Soul (God) of us."

> Satan creates problems on Earth and then when we become weak from trying to deal with these problems: Illness, war, gas prices and other injustices with things that you need to survive; then Satan whispers in your ears to woo you to his solutions for the problems. But you do not know these solutions will bring you more misery and cause you to end up in hell.

—God—received as this book was being written
"This is how His LORD knows of him, (meaning God knows that Satan is tempting us in this manner) for He sends His Angels along your path of crimes spent with Satan, in order for us of God (God's Angels), to get you through this ancient's evil torture toward mankind. (Satan's torture of mankind)

"But now God has sorrow of so much crime done upon His Earth, do to His adversary of pain more (Satan). He wishes Our child of God (me) show all of you that harm-of-self, when go to direction with evil souls is about to end for eternity sake. God will give your souls effort thus, with use of His Divine Core Angels by His side when His sons of Earth (mankind) call upon His heavenly Grace, LORD Jesus for end tyranny towards all mankind for sole means of putting God's power next to his own."

God declares war on Satan:
God has had enough of Satan's crimes on Earth and intends to stop him now. He wants me to show you that going in the direction of evil is about to end for the sake of eternity. God wants us to call Jesus, to end the tyranny from Satan on all mankind. This means call upon Jesus to put His power next to you when you need to fight Satan.

—God—received as this book was being written
"I have this much more, when God give strength, no evil of this Earth can stand against this strength. Power be with Our God against any foe for human kind. So don't give His Divine Soul just cause to leave Earth empty for us, that give His will upon souls lost from sin."

This means, don't give God cause to take the Angels from Earth and leave us with no defenses. With God by our side no evil can stand against this strength.

—God—received as this book was being written
"Give only love towards your God Almighty should heartache befall, or lesson made of evil call your name against Him."

Never say anything against God if you have heartache or if Satan has brought you pain or illness, only pray to God to help you and give only love to God. It is not God who is bringing you this pain, so don't let Satan teach you to say things against God.

—God—received as this book was being written
"For Almighty God have power enough without Angels strength also, to take away Earth forever more."

Even if God took all the Angels off of the Earth, He has the power to simply destroy Earth forever. So please don't give Him a reason.

23

Those Who Die Out of Grace

—Angel—original words of the plan
"I have seen of they who after no grace, die for God alone in bed of scorn for He. But no end of God is made of them; they spend eternity alone from God. No good of this will be. Only for lonely cause can souls be lost of God. Only for heart of soul is it right just of will for you to give His your strength way. Only in His way of good is anything possible after life is end."

—Angel—translated
I have seen what happens to those who die out of grace from God, who lie alone in bed with only scorn for God. But no end with God is made for them; they spend eternity alone from God. No good of this will be. Only by your own lonely cause can your soul be lost from God. So then, for no other reason than your own heart and soul and just cause for your will power, is it right for you to give God your life's strength. Only in God's way of good is anything possible after life has ended.

—Angel—original words of the plan
—Second listing for additional explanation by God
"Only for lonely cause can soul be lost of God. Only for heart of soul is it right just of will for you to give His your strength way. Only in His way of good is anything possible after life is end."

—God—explanation of the above received as this book was being written
"One can lose God, only when your lonely heart leaves its reason with God. **Remember God is holy; He is never able to see your world alone from His love of you.** You give back all love required of His being thus; without you to give this love to Him, the meaning of your creation would be incomplete. LORD has desire of only complete man of God. He gives life only to bring back love so chain of love between souls remains whole eternally."

You can only lose God when reasoning tells you there is no God. When God sees the world, He sees every one of us because of the love between Him and us. Our creation is a circle of love with God. He gives us love and then expects us to return that love. It was why He created us to begin with. So if you don't give God love in the manner that means love to God, then your creation remains incomplete. God will only allow complete men of God to enter Heaven. This circle of love is something God designed to continue for eternity.

—God—explanation of the above received as this book was being written
"***Just of will*** refers to a right form of grace to turn thy willpower toward. All power turned against God should give hopeless end for sinner who cast his will thus. None will be made of he who changes good will of God, for evil will with hell's sons based upon his fiery funeral place. All end justly."

> If you will God, you get Heaven; if you will Satan's way of life, you get hell. All end their life justly according to their will.

Amen, Amen I say unto you,
He has come your way today.
I bring His word for all of you,
Lest God walk over your way.

For He, His High awaits our souls,
In hope we get you see,
That Heaven's gate is not a swing,
But stay in hard a chain.

Is open not for those who say,
Our LORD be less of thee,
But gate is open more to thee,
When God becomes the sole of thee.

Lorenzo Ghiberti
1378-1455 Public Domain

24

Sadness of My Soul

—Angel—original words of the plan
"I know this is hard for you to say of this Carol, I know this end of much is sad of your soul this day. But however is spoken for thee it is more so for me."

—Angel—translated
I know it is hard for you to talk about this Carol. I know this end of many is sad for your soul this day. But however it hurts you, it is more so for me.

> The Angel was sympathizing with me because I got sad thinking about souls going to hell; and he said that even as much as it hurts me to see this happen, it hurts him even more.

25

God's Words Call Out Evil from its Hiding Place

—Angel—original words of the plan
"I have come only for this purpose. To give you/us all good will for our future if only we see our end is come with love of God first."

—Angel—translated
I have come only for this purpose. To give all of us good will for the future, if only we see our end of life has to come with love of God first.

—God—explanation of the above received as this book was being written
"This I say also, when others chase you around with swords pointed at your brain, give them My words with whole heart thus. For only of My word is evil called of his place of hiding to face God Almighty, with sword shining brightly of Heaven glow. None can combat against His might thus. Only God prevail of this end."

> When people come at you with words to tempt you to do wrong or tease you or criticize the good way you are trying to live, give them God's words whole heartedly and that will call out Satan from his hiding place to face God. Only God's words can call out Satan, and only God can fight him.

26

Give to Each Other

—Angel—original words of the plan
"Now I will talk about hope of will
This is no more than give of each other way. This is why He has send your heart
full with this task of ours, for He has seen your smile to Thee alone, for hope is
our heart's will of love."

—Angel—translated
This means no more than to give to each other. This is why God has made your
heart full with this task of ours, for God has seen your smile to Him alone, for
hope is our heart's will of love.

—Angel—original words of the plan
—Second listing for additional explanation by God
This means no more than give of each other way.

—God—explanation of the above received as this book was being written
"This means whenever you see someone in need, give them your help. It doesn't
mean only when you think about it or when it suits your purpose that day; it
means even if it inconveniences your life to do so. This way, you please Our
LORD very well, for nothing is too hard when God has asked it of you, and no
man belongs of himself on God's Earth. All have a responsibility to God when
someone of you needs service."

> This obviously doesn't mean for you to help others in need only when
> you can deduct it from your taxes. God expects the rich to help the
> poor of the Earth for no other reason than because it is the right thing
> to do. If God has graced your life with abundance, you are expected to
> share that with your fellow man. Remember, God has given all different
> abilities; your abilities helped you acquire wealth. Others never got your
> abilities, so for them to acquire the same wealth, would be impossible.

But they should be able to live a good life on God's Earth. Share in the beauty and nourishment that God provided to all mankind.

God planned for one to share with another in every way. Giving knowledge, food, clothing, a helpful hand to someone who is sick or old and needs something done in their home, etc.; and not hording what we have because we worked so hard for it, or we are afraid if we give to someone, more will ask us until they take all our money or all our time. God will see your gifts to others and know you are doing it in His honor. He will then give you more, because He trusts you to give to others what He gives you. If God sees you giving nothing, He will not give you anything either because you have not proven your ability to share.

Deuteronomy 24—**Moses**
19 When you are harvesting in your field and you overlook a sheaf, do not go back to get it. Leave it for the alien, the fatherless and the widow, so that the LORD your God may bless you in all the work of your hands. 20 When you beat the olives from your trees, do not go over the branches a second time. Leave what remains for the alien, the fatherless and the widow.

Matthew 25—**Jesus**
The Sheep and the Goats
31 "When the Son of Man comes in his glory, and all the angels with him, he will sit on his throne in heavenly glory. 32 All the nations will be gathered before him, and he will separate the people one from another as a shepherd separates the sheep from the goats. 33 He will put the sheep on his right and the goats on his left.

34 "Then the King will say to those on his right, 'Come, you who are blessed by my Father; take your inheritance, the kingdom prepared for you since the creation of the world. 35 For I was hungry and you gave me something to eat, I was thirsty and you gave me something to drink, I was a stranger and you invited me in, 36 I needed clothes and you clothed me, I was sick and you looked after me, I was in prison and you came to visit me.'

37 "Then the righteous will answer him, 'LORD, when did we see you hungry and feed you, or thirsty and give you something to drink? 38 When did we see you a stranger and invite you in or needing clothes and clothe you? 39 When did we see you sick or in prison and go to visit you?'

40 "The King will reply, 'I tell you the truth, whatever you did for one of the least of these brothers of mine, you did for me.'

41 "Then He will say to those on his left, 'Depart from me, you who are cursed, into the eternal fire prepared for the devil and his angels. 42 For I was hungry and you gave me nothing to eat, I was thirsty and you gave me nothing to drink, 43 I was a stranger and you did not invite me in, I needed clothes and you did not clothe me, I was sick and in prison and you did not look after me.'

44 "They also will answer, 'LORD, when did we see you hungry or thirsty or a stranger or needing clothes or sick or in prison, and did not help you?'

45 "He will reply, 'I tell you the truth, whatever you did not do for one of the least of these, you did not do for me.'

46 "Then they will go away to eternal punishment, but the righteous to eternal life."

Acts 20:35—**Paul**
In everything I did, I showed you that by this kind of hard work we must help the weak, remembering the words the LORD Jesus himself said: 'It is more blessed to give than to receive.'"

Luke 6—**Jesus**
35 But love your enemies, do good to them, and lend to them without expecting to get anything back. Then your reward will be great, and you will be sons of the Most High, because he is kind to the ungrateful and wicked. 36 Be merciful, just as your Father is merciful.

Luke 10—**Jesus**
The Parable of the Good Samaritan
25 On one occasion an expert in the law stood up to test Jesus. "Teacher," he asked, "what must I do to inherit eternal life?"

26 "What is written in the Law?" He replied. "How do you read it?"

27 He answered: "'Love the LORD your God with all your heart and with all your soul and with all your strength and with all your mind'; and, 'Love your neighbor as yourself.'"

28 "You have answered correctly," Jesus replied. "Do this and you will live."

29 But he wanted to justify himself, so he asked Jesus, "And who is my neighbor?"

30 In reply Jesus said: "A man was going down from Jerusalem to Jericho, when he fell into the hands of robbers. They stripped him of his clothes, beat him and went away, leaving him half dead. 31 A priest happened to be going down the same road, and when he saw the man, he passed by on the other side. 32 So too, a Levite, when he came to the place and saw him, passed by on the other side. 33 But a Samaritan, as he traveled, came where the man was; and when he saw him, he took pity on him. 34 He went to him and bandaged his wounds, pouring on oil and wine. Then he put the man on his own donkey, took him to an inn and took care of him. 35 The next day he took out two silver coins and gave them to the innkeeper. 'Look after him,' he said, 'and when I return, I will reimburse you for any extra expense you may have.' 36 "Which of these three do you think was a neighbor to the man who fell into the hands of robbers?"

37 The expert in the law replied, "The one who had mercy on him." Jesus told him, "Go and do likewise."

—Angel—original words of the plan
—Second listing for additional explanation by God
"This is why He has send your heart full with this task of ours, for He has seen your smile to Thee alone, for hope is our heart's will of love."

—God—explanation of the above received as this book was being written
"Our LORD comes to those who ask Him. Carol, God has seen the way you say prayers for yourself. He gives His blessing for all you pray for because your will of them whom you say prayers is that God give them His love through giving hope for them to see His Divine glory over their lives. So many pray selfish prayers for more things in their lives to come; only those of God's way say pray for hope with love for many.

"God has given this message so that all of Earth will bring His love with trust for His way help of thee, for each other to benefit with you. Give all Earth hope in a way of His Almighty God. Only when we say prayers, can this world change of its manner present, toward His LORD Almighty God. I want this plan to give more hope to Earth. This will give any who obey this present demand of faith with God all more courage and strength, toward ending evil upon Earth and getting God's souls toward His end with God's plan for them. Now all will know that Carol is choice of God for end evil upon Earth plan structure thus. She leads our way over all else because We with her have begun."

God wants all of us to benefit together from this plan. He wants me to give you help to know just how to do this plan, and he wants all of you to pray for me and help me, so that I can accomplish what God is asking me to do. (I really need your prayers, and I have been praying for all of you also.)

This plan was designed to bring hope to us on Earth, for a better life now; and a future without fear of evil for our children. If we all help each other to understand what God wants from us, in this demand for faith in only His will; then, we will help each other end our lives with God in Heaven. But most of all, we will fight along side our God to end evil on this Earth forever.

—God—received as this book was being written
"God Three Us (This is one way God refers to the Holy Trinity) have given this child My/Our blessed way forward to encourage souls toward God, so that evil (Satan) cannot send his evil self (David).

"I speak to My daughter in words God has chosen, for her ears can hear His minds thought through Our way of speech with her. To Us, with all Heaven, Carol is Our answer for giving the world Our way with God; so she has been given grace from God to know Our pattern in speech. So be always willing of her, so that she may give you God's will of all His Earth. Never think We of God did not give these phrases of Us to her; she has Our most highest blessing of her effort by Me, LORD God Almighty."

God speaks directly into my right ear, and sends me visions to emphasize his meaning. He has also given me dreams at night and visions during my prayer.

By the way, for artists who paint Jesus; He looks a little older than most paintings I have seen, and a little more weathered, but very much like the shroud. His skin tone is very tan; His hair is just below the ear line, not quite to the shoulder and dark brown. He describes His eyes as "clear as sun with blue highlights". So I would tell you, very crystal clear light gray with blue highlight and a twinkle, because he smiles a lot. And also, He is a little more muscular than most paint Him. Which makes sense to me, because he spent a lot of time as a carpenter while He was here.

One other important thing to note; God likes Jesus painted as the living LORD—not on the cross. God said, **"I want only His cross of resurrection shown; it never must give image, for Christ rose before Me."** He also would like Jesus pictured off the cross in churches, and said that He didn't approve of images of saints because people have

106

a tendency to pray to a saint for what they should be praying to God for. Of course that won't happen if you follow this plan and are asking God daily for all you need. God is the only one who answers prayers for those who ask correctly.

Numbers 12—Moses, words of God
6 "Listen to My words:
"When a prophet of the LORD is among you,
I reveal myself to him in visions,
I speak to him in dreams.

7 But this is not true of my servant Moses;
he is faithful in all my house.

8 With him I speak face to face,
clearly and not in riddles;

27

One Whose Black Heart Desires Quick Revenge

—Angel—original words of the plan
"Hope has many sides for Him. We have hope towards end of peace and grace of words. But now hope has meaning with love of souls that force our will towards evil males, or quick revenge desire of black in heart, with cold end aloof of only one man justice for Earth. He has given cold end of many who answer his call of praise to he."

—Angel—translated
Hope has many sides for God. We in Heaven, and you on Earth, have hope towards life's end in peace and grace of words. But now hope for us has a meaning with love of souls that force our will towards evil males, or one whose black heart desires quick revenge, and puts himself above others to give them a cold end, only for one man justice for Earth. This man has given a cold end to many who answer his call and have praise for him.

> God, and those in Heaven, hope that everyone on Earth end their life peacefully and in the grace of God. But now there is a man on Earth that is getting much attention in Heaven in regard to hope. This man's heart has blackened, with his desires for a quick revenge for others he considers beneath him. He has chosen one man justice as his answer to the people he is coldly and cruelly putting to death. Not only is he ending the lives of his enemy, but also those who have praised him as their leader.

> God wishes us not to be this man's judge so has not given his name. Only God is his judge. God wants him to realize on his own that he is the one God is talking about and to change his life to save his soul.

—God—explanation of the above received as this book was being written
"Hope for all of Earth means that at our end with this life, we end our days in graceful prayer to come to Our Father's home of Heaven. This is what every

person upon Earth thinks will be their end. Grace with peaceful sighs toward God's light upon our death.

"But many of Earth are now bringing one of God's men (a man on Earth) with earthbound foe (Satan), their unity and pleasure to serve his desire, weak with dark revenge of those he despises, because his mind and soul disagree of theirs.

"This man manages others over himself, by saying wrong answers to them about the right course of life for them. He sees only his desire and none with his heavenly Father's way for them. He produces weapons directed towards his hated victims. So now, his courageous followers give him fire-stroked (encouragement) as he gives orders to them to kill all who distress his thought for justice, among those he has claimed have been injured.

"Our man with this name, '**Evil Struck**'(name given him by Heaven), has killed many upon Earth for revenge theory given of him through his devil master; who has taken his good heart with love and replaces his thought desires with hatred of any who step away with distain toward his master being.

"His way will bring many of Our souls with God; toward evil end in hell, and give them good reward of Us instead."

> This man will tell people that they will get rewarded by God in Heaven, but instead they will end in hell for not asking God if what they are doing is God's will for them. You are being cautioned not to blindly follow someone of Earth who tells you to do anything against the laws of God. That man will not be the one to judge you when you die.

—God—continued

"Pray hard that this man sees his error ways. Bless be God of His kindness to wait alone of this man, for if his end is not rectified with God; all Earth will suffer his wrong mind plan."

> God wants all of us to pray for this man, so that he sees the error in what he is thinking. God is kindly waiting for this man to give up his freewill and humble himself to ask God what His will for his life really is. If this man doesn't go to God, all Earth will suffer from his wrong-thinking. There is much sadness in Heaven at what this man is doing. I want to add that God's energy became very sad as He was telling me about this man.

Proverbs 21—Solomon

14 A gift given in secret soothes anger,
and a bribe concealed in the cloak pacifies great wrath.

15 When justice is done, it brings joy to the
righteous but terror to evildoers.

16 A man who strays from the path of understanding
comes to rest in the company of the dead.

—God—received as this book was being written

"All Earth will know the terror of God, when those who go without His way in their hearts, refuse to give Almighty God first hand judgment of those who do not keep His Commandments."

God is letting us know that whatever terrorist plots against His children are created by mankind, they will not compare with the terror they (the terrorist) will know from God. Those who harm others for the sake of earthbound desires will face what God has in store for them. God's Commandments forbid killing and judging each other by standards of mankind. God alone will judge who is keeping His Commandments on Earth.

28

None with This Man's Heart Will See God

—Angel—original words of the plan
"I tell you for own safe retreat, that only this item/man has given cause of refrain/remorse to God's lips of stead. This soul's mind has warped along his way about scorning should be more his just revenge to those who place their trust upon his head."

—Angel—translated
I tell you for your own safe retreat, that only this man has given cause of refrain and remorse to God's lips right now. This soul's mind has warped along his way about how to handle those he has contempt or disdain for, who he considers despicable or unworthy. He thinks it should be more his just revenge to those who place their trust upon his head. (This man is on Earth now)

—God—received as this book was being written
"I wish also tell you that none with this man's heart—will see God upon death. He has been against God, to give others his reward on Earth. I say one other source with heart placed with evil dwell, can judge not what God's son alone has power over."

> This is very sad for me to say, but no one whose heart and mind are united with this man's way of thinking will see God when they die. In order to kill others the way he does and direct lives away from the plan God has for their lives; he has to be against God. No man of Earth can judge another man, for judgment of man is only the power of the Son of God, Jesus. It is evil to think you have this right. This is definitely not God's way for us to live.

—God—continued

"No man should let another of Earth give them God's judgment of their efforts on Earth in regard to prayer. Only God knows His will in regard of human effort thus."

> No man of Earth can tell another man of Earth what God will judge of his efforts regarding the way he prays to God. You are not allowed, by God, to tell anyone they are wrong in which religion they choose, or which prayers they say. Only God has this right to judge what is in each man's heart.

29

The Second Time Is Worse

—Angel—original words of the plan
"Second time is worse, for thee of little knowledge born in thee. He will give only good heart talk of thee, but in the end has sworn of thee, that end will grace his head with cord of stone cut from your soul."

Angel—translated
The second time is worse, for your descendants with little knowledge. The one who is coming will give only good-hearted talk to them; but in the end, has sworn to Satan that he will grace his head with cords of stone cut from their souls.

> The second time is referring to a time in the future, when Satan will send a man to Earth, who has sworn to take all souls left upon Earth to hell. This is referring to the coming of the antichrist who will call himself David, to mock God. Mankind will listen to him and think he is wonderful, but they will be fooled by his good-hearted talk. His only purpose on Earth will be to take souls to hell.

—God—explanation of the above received as this book was being written
"In our future Earth, we with no knowledge of this message about Heaven's evil enemy will have more complaint toward each other's souls. They will find easy hatred for others that take one bit of land away from them, or only small amounts placed in their hand, for many services and charms given them. These men of Earth cast doubt about anything said, for they will have loveless hearts lost with God's help toward them."

> The worst part about the coming of David will be the way people will act on Earth. Everything will be so bad here that there will be constant complaints about each other. There will only be loveless people left, and so no one will be able to find joy in anything they do. They will hate each other and argue over land and work and how much things cost. It will be even worse than the price of gas that has enraged all

of us these days. The reason for this hatred will be because God will not be around to bring love and safety to us against the evil that will take over Earth. If we do not follow this plan now, and give our love to God, in the manner He is asking us to give it to Him, then God will turn from us, as we have turned from Him.

—God—continued

"They (mankind) will give his evil source (David) their compliance word and force effort. His land of now is going to throw humans around like bounce off floors and walls (earthquakes, volcanoes, etc.). His (mankind) hope will ring strong against this force, but none with His LORD God will answer thus. All Earth will resent Our LORD for His refusal of their desires and needs. But God will see them away from His good self."

When God leaves the Earth to Satan; Satan will bring devastation on the people who are left on Earth. Earthquakes, volcanoes, tsunamis, it will feel like you are being tossed around Earth. People will pray to God, but it will be too late for them and God will not answer their prayers because they ignored Him when He asked for their love. There will only be hatred for God because He will look the other way when these souls call to Him for help.

—God—continued

"Nothing left with hope towards goodness will survive, after evil source (Satan) sends his man (David) upon Earth, to force them toward hell. This man with evil heart is sent only of Earth to give pains, after Earth gives of him their goals for future be. He will tell them good news of correct their errors thus, and condemn them after they take every good sign down for sake with he.

"None will see God, after this of God's enemy has given Earth his pledge toward giving Satan their souls. All have only his end."

This is painful to talk about; but all signs of God will disappear from Earth at the order of David. Those who are left will be ordered to worship David and be punished if they try to ask for God. What you may not realize is this: David will be able to know their thoughts, and will have the help of Satan and the power of his evil angels to punish them in the worst way if they think about God after they have given David their trust. No one on Earth will ever see God once David has pledged their souls to Satan. This is why it is so important for us to fight side-by-side with God now, against Satan, to change this end for mankind.

I realize this all sounds like some horrible science fiction movie, but it is real. It is written in the *Book of Revelations* in the Bible. You have to remember that what you are dealing with is spiritual and you have to use spirit of God to fight this. For those who live their lives saying they only believe in reality, I hate to be the one to burst your bubble, but your reality is based on delusion and your delusion is based on reality.

—Carol—original line from the plan
I asked, "Who are you speaking of?"

Gustave Dore 1833-1883 Public Domain

30

David

—Angel—original words of the plan
"I know his name on my lips is David. Man of so many souls end of his mind. David is our true end for those that have given this soul his part of history play. He is at the end of world history now. He has given his soul up again; for this is his end."

—Angel—translated
I know his name on my lips is David; a man who is thinking only about an end in hell for so many souls. David is our true end for those that have given this soul his part to play in history. He is at the end of world history now. He has given his soul up again; for this is his end.

—God—explanation of the above received as this book was being written
"David has been given Earth to destroy when all members of God have given him cause just. For when we say evil thoughts about God's plans for His children, and give evil-doers our desired efforts, instead of doing as Our LORD God commands His servants upon Earth should give Him; then Angels bound toward Earth will cease be, and angels of evil means can command Our LORD's souls (us) away from He. Earth will perish so, if David comes upon it. For God will not step against him, when only good on Earth have chosen David. God will spend not one instant of time again—toward souls that give His enemy power thus."

This is extremely important to realize; God wants your love; that is why you were created. If you give your love to Satan, with the acts you do on this Earth, then you create your own end. It is your freewill to choose against God. Heaven is a place of pure love. You cannot get to Heaven if you choose to ignore what God is asking you to do now. God said that only through knowing His will for you, will you know how to love God the way He wants you to love Him. Talk against God or His plan to save you and He will take the Angels to Heaven and leave Earth to the fallen angels. God will not spend one instant of time again—towards souls that give Satan power.

Also let me make this perfectly clear to anyone who is selfish and thinks their individual will is not going to harm anyone but themselves. This is a prelude to the end of the world laid out in the Bible. So what you do now, what all of us do now, is affecting everyone on Earth, and any who would follow us. This is no time to be selfish; **if you love anyone at all, it is their end you are responsible for, along with your own.**

Exodus 17:2—**Moses**
So they quarreled with Moses and said, "Give us water that we may drink" And Moses said to them, "Why do you quarrel with me? Why do you test the LORD?"

Matthew 4:7—**Jesus**
Jesus answered him, "It is also written: 'Do not put the Lord your God to the test.'"

—**God**—continued
"David has agreed to Satan that in the end his time with God's soul will vanish, all Earth will know his strength because he will take each man's soul to Lucifer. All in hell will see his true source. Only Heaven will condemn him, but Earth will glorify his name among their own. All will see him as God's forced man against good. So God has deemed his soul will vanish all else. No end will be made of him; only gone forever more."

> David won't go to hell; God will vanish his soul completely for the evil he will do.

—**God**—continued
"This man will name God as his own LORD. He will say Our God is my name. He will give hope to those who praise him. All Earth will know him as the true lamb with Father, son of His Most High. His heart will appear good as shown; his only weapon against Us will be his tongue, blazing of fire. All can see his torment of any who disobey his orders for them. None will survive when his name said of them. He has given Us Our say, and will close off Our people of Us, when they come of him, instead of Us."

> This man will say he is from God and is God, and when he has convinced all that he is good, those on Earth will begin to see his evil deeds and no one will be able to stop him. He will torment any who try. No one

will survive if they say his name in place of Our true God. They will be marked by David.

Satan is giving Heaven their say with this plan, but if we don't choose God then it will close us off from Heaven's help because we chose Satan instead of God. God will not come to our aid if we have chosen Satan over him. God chooses to be in the company of the good. Believe me; Satan is going to be fighting this plan. Things on Earth are going to get worse before they get better. I promise you Earth is going to become a battle ground for good and evil like we have never seen before.

—Carol—original line from the plan
I asked, "Is David on Earth now?"

31

Evil Dwells of David Now

—Angel—original words of the plan
"He's send only for many of years ahead. But he has agreed to this end advance, to become his slave; for evil dwell of David now."

—Angel—translated
He will be sent for many years from now. But he has agreed in advance, to become Satan's slave; for evil dwells in David now.

—God—explanation of the above received as this book was being written
"Evil has taken many forms over the years since God has cast his soul to Earth. This man that once has been alone of Earth crust is not gone. His soul waits until Earth will have source full of loathing of God, before his spirit more appears to you again. In his present state he lives of hell, but once you can give him reason, his being will come as his enemy with devil and give God's home of Heaven as his way toward take hold of hearts. His name of Earth has struck cord with His Almighty God, for he chooses Great King to criticize against Our LORD's command for him."

> This soul we are calling David was once a man on Earth, who is filled with hatred for God and mankind. His soul waits in hell for another chance to come back and get revenge on Earth, by bringing souls to Lucifer. He has picked the name David because he knows it will anger God. God has allowed Lucifer to bring David to Earth if we choose to give our love to the things Satan wants us to do and take our love away from God.

> God has changed the timing of the statement above. He now gives us twelve years to comply with His plan, but if we don't comply, He will allow Satan to bring David.

—God—continued

"None who take heed of him will see God and know Heaven; for he of evil source, bound us to his course of action, if none born of Earth give Us Our will for own will."

> If we of Earth don't give God our will to be replaced with His will for us, then we give David his course to take action against us. This was an agreement between Lucifer and God when Lucifer was cast to Earth. If man chooses evil instead of God, then God would let Lucifer take our souls because we of our freewill have chosen against God.
>
> We were given freewill as part of this agreement between God and Lucifer. This is how you know that Lucifer was on Earth before mankind. So this has been an ongoing battle since Adam and Eve. Can you imagine how God felt when the first two people He put on Earth committed the first offense against Him. God keeps fighting for our love, and sees the state of this Earth, and knows that right now, He is not winning. We would rather give in to the pleasures of Earth (Lucifer's domain) than offer our freewill to God and do as God commanded us to do.
>
> The reason God will give David the Earth is because ultimately, God will win and He will use Lucifer and David as a means to show all His power over evil, and show His Almighty glory. (Of course this part may not be for a long, long time after Earth ends. You will be in hell if you refuse God. Remember, God has eternity to spring you out of that jail. Remember also, God created Lucifer and the fallen angels and sent them onto the Earth. They only exist because of Him; they only live now because of His love for them.)
>
> God is hoping that mankind will not force Him to this end. He wants us to love Him enough to show Satan here and now that we choose Him (God) over evil. God does love us enough to change the end of the world and it's up to us to show God we love Him enough to change it with Him. God also wants mankind to have a time on His good Earth when we can live peacefully and in the manner He planned for us all along.

—God—continued

"Only of this evil man can Earth die of Us. Go give Our loved Earth, God's plan for stopping David. I beseech all of you, pray against this end. It will bring hatred so great against God and The LORD will strike down Satan upon his soul's revenge with man."

Pray that the LORD's plan is followed or Satan will bring great hatred against God until the LORD strikes him down for what he will do to those left on Earth.

—Carol—original line from the plan
I said, "This is kind of frightening. I am afraid to put this in this book for fear that people will discredit all the good you are saying."

Pietro di Cristoforo 1450-1523 Public Domain

Prayer When Others Are Trying to Harm You

Have only one thought when all hope is bad,
That God is here of your side.
When only he who irritates thee
Is near of thee again.

Should only have Our God for way,
When blessed with trust abates for thee,
Have just your LORD in heart of soul
When never hear your words.

For God alone give right/just for you,
And tear in others place.
For He alone will justify
A longing of your face.

Save only just cause against all others
Who scorn for humors sake,
And bless thee in God's name of more
When tossed against the fence.

And say of them who hurt your side
When others have agitate,
That left alone, away from God
Is now a way of hate.

Be quiet in pain for He will see
That your mind is left of He,
That gives you strength to fight against
All welcome tyranny.

He chase your foes away for thee
When say the rosary.

32

Just Cause to Change Earth

—Angel—original words of the plan
"Listen of me now, for in the end I have only given just cause for you to make changes needed for stop his coming. Earth has not end this way now. He has no charge of you over God. He is only come when he has charge, because you choose just cause for him and lose respect of cause of His LORD."

—Angel (rather sternly)—translated
Listen to me now, for in the end I have only given you just cause for you to make changes needed to stop David's coming. Earth has not ended this way yet. Satan has no charge of you over God. He can only come when he has charge, because you choose a just cause for him and lose respect for your cause of Our LORD.

> God gave us this plan to change history, to change what was written in the Bible. He has watched what Lucifer has done to mankind and wants to stop him now.
>
> Without God's intervention through prophets or speaking to us directly, we have fallen away from His laws or changed them to justify what we want to do. But His love for us is so great that He wants to stop what Satan is doing to us (the unknowing ones, the blind ones).
>
> At this time, God is still trying to save as many souls as He can. That was His one order to me, "Go and save as many as you can." I cried of course, wondering how one little woman was going to make a big enough noise to shake up the Earth. But I have God with me and He has a huge voice.
>
> Right now, Satan does not have control; even though, looking around this Earth, it sure does look like he has a large hold on a huge number of people. But God is still in charge and we all still have an Angel with us 24/till we die. Unless the number of people who are falling into

Satan's power changes and enough people turn to God through this plan, David will be given the right to come.

—God—received as this book was being written
"I add this much: I will bless any of you who end the coming of his evil soul. I will take all who fight for love with God, over end of David's plan against God, to a place of peace, within walls so glorious that you will never worry again that your life here was over. This, I promise My people. I, LORD of all universe and more, have commanded this child of mine to give you Our will for your life against evil more. So never say against her soul/heart, for she with We have come only with purpose toward saving Earth from hell's end."

God tells us many times in this book about the blessings we will get if we follow this plan. Let me assure you that no one on Earth can offer you a place in Heaven, so don't let someone on Earth convince you that following God into this battle is a bad thing to do.

It's so kind of God to ask people not to speak against me. To be sure, this is a tough spot to be in. I know that Satan will be working overtime to make me look bad because he doesn't want me helping God to save souls. God will deal with Satan one-on-one, when enough of mankind has joined this fight for us to be able to show Satan that God has all the power and all our love.

Also, I am sure there will be a lot of people who currently have some amount of earthly power, who will not want to lose any of it, and a lot of people making a great deal of money under the guide of Satan, that will not want to see business drop. So I anticipate a huge fight with Satan and could use as many people on God's side as possible. In this war with the Devil, there is no way to be on God's side and still do Satan's bidding. So either you are with God, or you are not.

Proverbs 14—Solomon
11 The house of the wicked will be destroyed,
but the tent of the upright will flourish.

12 There is a way that seems right to a man,
but in the end it leads to death.

13 Even in laughter the heart may ache,
and joy may end in grief.

Unknown Artist, Public Domain

33

Save Our God's Name in the Hearts of Man

—Angel—original words of the plan
"Let make clear our progress here. I have come of love for you/God, so that Earth has chance for save our God's name, in hearts of man. Only truth of future's end can change our mind's heart of present form for life."

—Angel—translated
Let's make clear our progress here. I have come out of love for you and God so that Earth has a chance to save our God's name, in the hearts of man. Only the truth of the future's end can change your minds and hearts, from this present form of life.

—Angel—original words of the plan
—Second listing for additional explanation by God
"Only truth of future's end can change our mind's heart of present form for life."

—God—explanation of the above received as this book was being written
"You cannot give up your present sinful doings of this life without knowing that Our LORD God is angry about the way His Earth is greeting His enemy. If none will fight evil as God commands, then Earth will end sooner. God has not given you details for reasons more His own; but God will not let Satan win your souls if you ask His way of life for you. He waits a long time, only to let you give His soul your respect of love and trust. **Then all Earth can live with peaceful bliss toward God who will give further life to your planet. This I promise My souls with mankind hearts filled with love of God."**

> God is angry about the way we are giving in to Satan. This is the reason that He has chosen to fight Satan now. If you are giving up your sinful doings, it has to be because you know how angry God is and you are ready to fight on His side. But God will wait until you give Him your freewill and ask for His will for you, before He considers you a member in His Army; because only then do you show God respect, love and trust. If enough people don't join, God will end Earth sooner. But if

we fight evil with God, the Earth will live on and God promises us abundance like never before.

I feel I need to clarify one point for you. You were given freewill so that you could choose between God and Satan [Good and evil]. By giving God your freewill, you are saying to God, "I give up my will and my right to choose evil." Then, and only then are you able to give all your love to God. If you hang on to your freewill, you are hanging on to your will to choose Satan. How then can you say you love God? You cannot serve two masters.

—God—continued

"All mankind needs to know about how much more loyal His LORD God is about their lives, then they currently understand. But God has more love around them than any could understand. This is only of Heaven's knowing, for Earth can not foresee His power towards them."

There are things about the way God shows love to mankind that are hidden from us. If God showed us how He protects us, He would also have to show us the evil around us that He is protecting us from. Also, God has planned our lives to fit with the lives of all else on Earth. However, Satan interferes with this plan and brings man against man for purposes of earthly pleasures that will not last.

Think about it, when you gain pleasure on Earth based from an evil means, you not only lose that pleasure, but you lose part of yourself. Nothing gained with Satan lasts for very long. That is because nothing gained with Satan is based in love and honor, and in praise of the LORD. So why would it last, if our purpose on Earth is to complete a circle of love with God? Therefore, things gained through Satan have no real purpose in your life but to bring instant gratification, and will disappear as fast as they come; they have nothing to sustain them. Satan really doesn't want you to have sustained happiness and a good life.

Proverbs 16—Solomon
3 Commit to the LORD whatever you do,
and your plans will succeed.

4 The LORD works out everything for his own ends
—even the wicked for a day of disaster.

5 The LORD detests all the proud of heart.
Be sure of this: They will not go unpunished.

34

This Is Not Forlorn of Time;
It Is a Forewarning of Time

—Angel—original words of the plan

"This is not forlorn of time spread; is forewarn time. Let us know that he is with us only if he give us his evil cause for good. We can banish his cause if known to us how Our LORD has changed this scorned plan, to our behalf. See this is not done in grief of soul; it is done for save your Earth plan now."

—Angel—translated

This is not for you to despair about the future; it is a time to forewarn of it, to let you know that David can only be with us if Satan gives us his evil course for good. We can banish Satan's cause if it is known to us how *Our LORD has changed Satan's scorned plan on our behalf*. See, this is not done in grief to your souls; it is done to save your Earth plan now.

—God—received as this book was being written

"I say this now, God requires you give more time to Him than ever before in history of this Earth. You must say Morning Prayer with His LORD, only for cause against evil spirits around your minds and hearts each moment in the day. God sees Satan's evil plan against you, knows his answer when you give him heed of you, and will stop him (Satan) when you ask Him (God) to bring you out of Satan's evil traps. You will never know the extent of danger your souls will be in, when Satan brings his most hated soul (David) back toward Earth. Only God and we above can see this devastation brewing in advance, and only through help from God, can you bear this revenge plan toward Earth that Satan aimed at your end with hell. Now, no one will be safe, unless you give your love and hearts toward God for safety sake. Only God can end his (Satan's) justice plan against God Almighty, because Satan is still of God's end for him."

God can end Satan's plan if we all ask His help, and Satan knows that God has his end planned. Currently this world has a lot of middle-of-the-road religious. We go to church, chant our prayers, and leave until the next week, or don't show up at church at all, giving little or no thought of God in between. But we say we love God, and pray whenever we need His help.

Well this is God asking for our help; and God is telling us that there is no middle-of-the-road in this fight with Satan. There is no one religion that is being called to help God. God is calling all mankind this time in history, to save our Earth from the coming of David and the end of the world. There is no time left to quibble over whose religion is right or wrong, or whose government is right or wrong, or who should own what lands. There is no time left to pick which color skin is best, or if men are better than women, or who has the bigger bombs or greater power. God has all the power and He intends on using it to save us, if we join Him in this fight.

To be on God's side we have to give all the means of Satan up that we have been using for centuries. This is not going to be easy, but we don't really have much choice. We are the generation God picked to do this. We have to offer up our free will to choose for ourselves what kind of lives we want; and let God tell us what kind of life we were meant to have when He created us. So, for some on this Earth, life won't change much, but for others life will change dramatically.

God told me that David's coming is stated in the Bible, in *The Book of Revelations*. This new plan of God's is to change what is written in the Bible as per God's will of now. God is doing this to save Earth because of His love for us and to end His pain at seeing what Satan is doing to us.

—Carol—comment from original message
I have learned in the last ten years that Angels will only say truth and they don't pull punches to protect our sensitive minds. They come to help, and their messages aren't always easy to want to hear. There are many times I have walked away from my computer and shut down my thoughts because of my fears. But I made a commitment to God to tell you everything I hear, and God is holding me to my promise.

35

Give Thought to What We Have to Do

—Angel—original words of the plan

"*So let's give mind to what we have/should do, in view of what I have made clear this day.*"

—Angel—translated

So let's give some thought to what we have to do in view of what I have made clear this day.

Send wish to God, see of many warn,
For He will end you free.
For God is left of many
Who have wreck in test of thee.

So for now I say in mind of soul,
You can foretell of true,
If only then is where you go/see
Then soul will get you Thee.

36

Satan Has a Plan to Take Our Lives

—Angel—original words of the plan
"None of us are willing of self, to throw away our homes and children of future day. We pray for only this day's journey to be graced with love for joys with God; however this, we must/will pray of then to come with more zest of give in heart."

—Angel—translated
None of us are willing in spirit, to throw away the homes and children of the future. We pray for the future's children, to be graced with love for joy with God; however, we must pray for them with more zest of heart.

—God—explanation of the above received as this book was being written
"We can not ask ourselves as good God-loving people, to let our homes and children be forsaken, when we can do what we need to do now, to protect their lives. We fight all our lives for those we care about and love, and never let harm come to anyone of our children if at all possible. Now God is telling you that what you do today directly affects the lives of your own children and your children's, children. They will suffer if you don't change your course of life on Earth.

"You can not continue to live in sinful abandon, while Satan has a plan to take your children's lives away from God. Your cause will change evil. Your way is not going to give God His rightful do if it doesn't change now. God is our Savior and is our way, if we change course of this, He will abandon His Earth to Satan. God will not let us give Satan His love and give us another chance. This is our chance to prove our loyalty to His Divine Spirit."

> We can not give Satan our will now and the love that belongs only to God and disregard the command of God in this plan, and expect God to give us another chance. This plan is telling you that this is your chance to save yourself and your children to come. There is not another time to do this, and no more time left. You can both give God your love and ask His will for you or you lose everything.

—God—continued

"I wish my people understand that it pains My soul to ask for your love and will be shared of Mine with you. In all of time against us of Earth soul's form (from Adam and Eve until now), not one of Earth wishes My soul comfort toward My will over them. All have found this hard of will to give toward Me. Even of saints form of glory be, they with Earth have punish My soul; with argue more over thoughts formed of will for them. All have prayed for end in less distress than willed of them. All accept none of truth, without hopeless want for less suffer of they, against Earth's denials toward our value just reward. I with LORD (The Holy Trinity) will end Our pain of this when Earth is again vanished this Satan soul. Then God can rest His soul in peace once more. All mankind will no longer have evil to justify for them—His pained being."

> I don't know about the rest of you, but the statement above from God has completely humbled me. I found myself sobbing for all the pain God has had to endure from His loved souls, since the beginning of mankind (Adam and Eve).
>
> We just don't think about how Almighty God feels when we offend Him, by not asking what He would like us to do for Him. We are so selfish with our pride and freewill that we never consider what God needs from us; we only give thought to what this powerful, loving being . . . can do for us.
>
> Well, God is telling us right here that it pains Him that He even has to ask us to love Him, and ask His will for us. We who He created should have learned this in all these years on Earth. How it would pain us if our very own children never asked us what we needed; if we never saw them do our will without doubt or grumbling about it. If not even once we got that love and respect from them. How much more is Our LORD pained from His children in the billions and billions created? What a devastating thought this is.
>
> I guess we think if we ask His will, He is going to ask something hard of us to do. I assure you He is, but He will also give you everything you need to do His will. You will never be on your own to complete anything God asks you to do. And yes, He is going to ask you to change from your evil ways and be good. And yes, it is not going to be easy at all to do this. But one thing that all of us on Earth have discovered in all our years here is when we join together for a cause and all of us are struggling together to achieve a goal, then any effort becomes the efforts of all. This is what will make this whole plan work for us. We

are united in our effort to love God, the way God deserved to be love from the beginning.

What a loving God we have; for Him to have waited all this time for us to give Him the honor and praise and love He so justly deserves from us. God has asked us in such a humble way, by offering us safe haven from our enemy, and by taking our enemy from Earth and presenting us everlasting love and life, as a means of easing His pain.

How can anyone possibly deny this love? I only wish I could share with all of you the energy God surrounds me with, because then you would all understand His love for us. I wish I could share the pain and sorrow God and Jesus let me feel as they talk about the way mankind turns to Satan and away from them.

God is so powerful and so holy and right in everything. But with us, His children, He is like a giant who sees a tiny feather fall off a small bird and gently bends to get it and secure it back on the wing again.

37

Don't Throw This Knowledge Away Out of Fear

—Angel—original words of the plan
"I pray you see this holy way towards your save Earth's plan; then throw this knows away for sakes of fear and woe in tears of pain within."

—Angel—translated
I pray you can see this is God's holy way of giving you a plan to save your Earth, rather than throw this knowledge away for the sake of fear and woes in tears of pain within.

—God—received as this book was being written
"Tears and woe will come when those who look away of this plan; criticize and make fun of those who want Our LORD's way plan to change Earth. All will not accept this way of life. Many will fear change to what they have been used to and many more will hold on to wealth with greed, instead of a course with love toward God. God is patient, and gives many more His answer, before all will come of Him. But let it be said, that when nothing moves your heart toward His LORD, He will send Angels to give hope for those who suffer under your test of them. He will give mercy only toward those who give His soul love each day, and work toward His plan. But for those who criticize them, He will give hardships to convince your heart to give courage of this plan, your power."

—God
"The LORD trusts that His children will give Him their just love and respect needed to give Satan terror in his soul. This is God's will of all Earth; no man or woman of any nation is beyond this call. No religion banded, no race agreed safe. God gives this order; a new command is now, one that requires all Earth to participate equally.

"All leaders should heed my warning of this day—for I will cancel your power in seconds, if you once give orders against Me.
I, LORD of all, have given this message."

—God

"All Earth is equal in God's eyes. No man will come before Me without judgment given his ways toward others in his care upon Earth. So before you even lift one finger of yours against another son with God; I say this, I will come down hard against your life should harm be made toward those who have done nothing of Me wrong. I have given man all of Earth, only for the purpose of living out life; not to give wrong working with mankind against man."

> God did not give us Earth so that we could fight over property and differences of ways or cultures.

—God

"All fighting with way, need My blessing only."

> God is saying if you are going to fight about your different ways, you need His blessing first or you cannot fight. So here's your solution. In order to hear God's answer, you have to give up your freewill for God's will of you. God's will as described in this plan is not to fight. It seems God has caught you in a technicality. I told you, He is very clever.

—God

"When I have no word from man regarding My will for this, then fighting is done with mankind course alone."

> If you fight without going to God regarding your differences, then you are doing it against the will of God and using only your own will.

—God

"Any who punish My people of Earth, should know I have their end in hand. I will give them the way they gave other souls brought before them. I say this of all course taken against mankind; either large scale war or one against another argue the same."

> God will treat you the way you treat anyone brought before you, if you punish, he will punish you. This is in regard to any fighting be it war or between two people.

—God

"I will be there whenever man has course of another. All must give of Me only, so I can judge his end. This is what LORD of all Heaven, with souls come daily, has given word of those left aside in planet Earth."

God tells us that He is the only one who judges another. Any time one man has a grievance with another; God is there to judge both. If we take action against our foes, we take away God's will of the situation. The LORD judges all who die daily and those who are left on Earth must let Him judge the rest of what is done on Earth.

—God
"All judgment is Mine to give. Be careful to heed Our warning to this end. Now is not a time of wonder; *it is time for atonement of sins given thus far*. All Earth is need with Me by their side only.

I have placed sin with spirit thus, as whole agenda course thus far now. # War of Earth with Satan is now. **No one has stronger reason to fight against this evil source than one of Me. I will say when enough are involved and when only Earth survives Us."**

God has made our fight against Satan His priority; no one has a stronger reason to take up this fight, than the love of God. This is not a time to be fighting with each other; it is a time to be fighting against Satan, along side our God, through love of each other. If you are fighting each other, God has your end planned for you, because you are not doing His will. His will is that you fight the fight He wants you to fight, in the manner He has chosen—through love.

—God
"Give praise of Our LORD who has accepted your pains and punishment thus of His soul; who gives you love, in place of scorn for your behavior of Him."

I picked these next Bible passages because I love the way they show the power of God. They also have a lot of similarities to what God is doing today.

Isaiah 13—Isaiah
1 An oracle concerning Babylon that Isaiah son of Amoz saw:

2 Raise a banner on a bare hilltop, shout to them;
beckon to them to enter the gates of the nobles.

3 I have commanded my holy ones;
I have summoned my warriors to carry out my wrath—
those who rejoice in my triumph.

4 Listen, a noise on the mountains,
like that of a great multitude!
Listen, an uproar among the kingdoms,
like nations massing together!
The LORD Almighty is mustering an army for war.

5 They come from faraway lands,
from the ends of the heavens—
the LORD and the weapons of his wrath—
to destroy the whole country.

6 Wail, for the day of the LORD is near;
it will come like destruction from the Almighty.

7 Because of this, all hands will go limp;
every man's heart will melt.

8 Terror will seize them, pain and anguish will grip them;
they will writhe like a woman in labor.
They will look aghast at each other,
their faces aflame.

9 See, the day of the LORD is coming—
a cruel day, with wrath and fierce anger—
to make the land desolate and destroy the sinners within it.

10 The stars of heaven and their constellations will not show their light.
The rising sun will be darkened and the moon will not give its light.

11 I will punish the world for its evil,
the wicked for their sins.
I will put an end to the arrogance of the haughty
and will humble the pride of the ruthless.

12 I will make man scarcer than pure gold,
more rare than the gold of Ophir.

13 Therefore I will make the heavens tremble;
and the Earth will shake from its place
at the wrath of the LORD Almighty,
in the day of his burning anger.

14 Like a hunted gazelle,
like sheep without a shepherd,
each will return to his own people,
each will flee to his native land.

15 Whoever is captured will be thrust through;
all who are caught will fall by the sword.

I like to think of this as God capturing Satan and the evil angels.

16 Their infants will be dashed to pieces before their eyes;
their houses will be looted and their wives ravished.

17 See, I will stir up against them the Medes,
who do not care for silver and have no delight in gold.

I like to think of the Medes as us and the Angels. Together, we will strike down all that Satan has done. No matter what Satan holds up in front of us, we will see through his trickery.

18 Their bows will strike down the young men;
they will have no mercy on infants
nor will they look with compassion on children.

19 Babylon, the jewel of kingdoms,
the glory of the Babylonians' pride,
will be overthrown by God like Sodom and Gomorrah.

I think of Babylonian pride as Satan's pride overthrown because even in the days of Babylon, Sodom and Gomorrah it was Satan who drove those people to sin so badly that God destroyed the cities. ***Now God wishes to destroy the cause of sin; not the effect of sin.***

20 She will never be inhabited or
lived in through all generations;
no Arab will pitch his tent there,
no shepherd will rest his flocks there.

21 But desert creatures will lie there,
jackals will fill her houses there the owls will dwell,
and there the wild goats will leap about.

138

22 Hyenas will howl in her strongholds,
jackals in her luxurious palaces.
Her time is at hand, and her days will not be prolonged.

I think of this as the end of our desire to do the will of Satan. No one who loves God will want to be associated with evil ever again. Satan will be considered a desolate land.

Isaiah 14
1 The LORD will have compassion on Jacob;
once again he will choose Israel
and will settle them in their own land.
Aliens will join them and unite with the house of Jacob.

2 Nations will take them and bring them to their own place.
And the house of Israel will possess the nations
as menservants and maidservants in the LORD's land.
They will make captives of their captors
and rule over their oppressors.

Here, realize that the house of Jacob for us today is referring to the way these people obeyed God. **United as one people.** *They were a nation doing God's will no matter how hard it got, because God told them they were the chosen people. Today God is telling us we are to join Israel is this manner. God is choosing all of us today to follow His will, and to join His fight. You might say God is telling us we are all united with the house of Jacob, because today we are all expected to do the will of God, no questions asked.*

Menservants and maidservants in the LORD's land today are all of us serving the LORD. Our captives are the evil dwellers on Earth; Satan, our oppressor.

3 On the day the LORD gives you relief from suffering
and turmoil and cruel bondage (from Satan),

4 you will take up this taunt against the king of Babylon:
How the oppressor has come to an end!
How his fury has ended!

5 The LORD has broken the rod of the wicked,
the scepter of the rulers,

6 which in anger struck down people with unceasing blows,
and in fury subdued nations with relentless aggression.

7 All the lands are at rest and at peace;
they break into singing.

8 Even the pine trees and the cedars of Lebanon
exult over you and say, "Now that you have been laid low,
no woodsman comes to cut us down."

9 The grave below is all astir to meet you at your coming;
it rouses the spirits of the departed to greet you—
all those who were leaders in the world;
it makes them rise from their thrones—
all those who were kings over the nations.

I can tell you that the day the Son of God comes to ask us if we are ready to do the will of God; you will see the Earth as it truly is. No evil will be kept from your site. Spirits of the dead will be in full view. It will be a frightening day for all who are here. But God's purpose in showing us all this will be to allow any who have not come to fight Satan with the rest of us, a chance to see what the alternative really is. God knows that once you see evil around you, you will have no doubts or objections to join our fight.

10 They will all respond, they will say to you,
"You also have become weak, as we are;
you have become like us.

11 All your pomp has been brought down to the grave,
along with the noise of your harps;
maggots are spread out beneath you and worms cover you.

12 **How you have fallen from Heaven,
O morning star,
son of the dawn you have been cast down to the Earth,
you who once laid low the nations!**

13 You said in your heart,
"I will ascend to Heaven;
I will raise my throne above the stars of God;
I will sit enthroned on the mount of assembly,
on the utmost heights of the sacred mountain.

14 I will ascend above the tops of the clouds;
I will make myself like the Most High."

15 But you are brought down
to the grave, to the depths of the pit.

16 Those who see you stare at you, they ponder your fate:
"Is this the man who shook the Earth and made kingdoms tremble,

17 the man who made the world a desert,
who overthrew its cities and would not let his captives go home?"

18 All the kings of the nations lie in state each in his own tomb.

19 But you are cast out of your tomb like a rejected branch;
you are covered with the slain,
with those pierced by the sword,
those who descend to the stones of the pit.
Like a corpse trampled underfoot,

20 you will not join them in burial,
for you have destroyed your land and killed your people.
The offspring of the wicked will never be mentioned again.

21 Prepare a place to slaughter his sons
for the sins of their forefathers;
they are not to rise to inherit the land
and cover the Earth with their cities.

22 **"I will rise up against them,"**
declares the LORD Almighty.
"I will cut off from Babylon her name and survivors,
her offspring and descendants," declares the LORD.

23 "I will turn her into a place for owls and into swampland;
I will sweep her with the broom of destruction,"
declares the LORD Almighty.

God has no intention of letting Satan win our souls. God intends to use us to show Satan that mankind will not let Our God down. We will fight by Our LORD's side and win our Earth back and show him that we love God above all else.

Let me tell you why I picked these last two Bible passages. It is not because I felt they were describing this plan or Satan's plan to bring David. Although an awful lot of the lines surely do become familiar again. I picked them because I fell in love with the power of God in these words. I felt they showed how others in history saw the way God brought people together to fight against evil. I wanted us to remember that God is with us, whenever there is a fight to be had against Satan's evil deeds.

You see also in these lines the love of God, when it is told of how once evil is taken off the Earth, all is good again and all will be able to live peacefully. Throughout history, man has fought against man because of Satan; but this time in our history, man will fight alongside of our God against Satan. And for the first time in our planet's history since Adam and Eve; this Earth will be blessed by God to be the way it was in the beginning. For very many of us, it will be in our lifetime, and in our children's lifetime. We are fighting for our Earth, our lives, and our children's lives. But most of all, we are fighting for a God who has been waiting century upon century to bring peace to His soul. What more honored cause can you have than to give back to God what is rightfully His—The love and praise of all mankind.

Shonda Reneal © 1998-2006 by ReneaL™

38

Honest and Truth Is Brought to You

—Angel—original words of the plan
"Honest and truth is brought of you this morning child; for glow in hand is only God's plan and step on souls is no truth or plan. Have faith of thee in more to life's wonder, when Earth shall live of thee make so. Only for future child, take thought of cord that strangles heart's souls towards bitter end."

—Angel—translated
Honesty and truth is brought to you this morning, child, because healing the Earth is only God's plan; and one (Satan) who would stomp on your soul, in not truth or a plan for you. You can have faith that your world will see more of life's wonders, and Earth shall live on, because you have made it so by following this plan. Only for the future's child, think about the cord that strangles souls towards a bitter end (Satan's plan).

> Sometimes truth is staring us right in the face, but we don't want to believe it, because if we do so, it means that we have to make an effort, not only to step out of our little box of safety that we create for ourselves, but we have to get rid of the box completely. So we choose to ignore what we can describe as inappropriate for our life.
>
> This book is about a truth that would frighten anyone; it's about a subject that is so controversial that it has caused people to fight and go to war since the beginning of mankind. 'What God wants' from us.
>
> God tried to let us know in the holy book; He issued orders the way he wanted them carried out. But man has had an invisible enemy on Earth who has tormented us, stepped on our dreams of living the abundant life God provided for us, and in our ignorance of this enemy's power over our thoughts, we continue to blame each other for misfortunes due to misunderstanding God's laws, instead of putting the blame on Satan, where it belongs.

God is telling you now, that Satan strangles your soul until it is so loveless for ourselves, our fellow man and for God, that he can easily convince us to do the wrong thing. To blame your brother for your problems, to steal, to cheat, to commit adultery, to kill, dishonor your parents, and most of all, to turn away from God.

This evil Satan has convinced people that God is not helping them, that God is causing disease and earthquakes and so on; and that God does the things that are destroying lives. He has convinced people that God chooses to punish mankind for their sins. But **God does not.**

God sent Jesus to Earth to forgive sin, so why would God still be punishing man? He sent Jesus to teach us how to live, so why would God do things that would cause our death? God even gave us, through Jesus, a religion that above all, teaches forgiveness and loving each other.

No where, in anything Jesus said, is there one statement to tell us to harm each other for any reason. He never once said to verbally or physically harm your fellow man, if that man does not agree with you. So, I for one am completely confused about holy wars and repressing religions. I understood from reading the holy book that only God has a right to judge mankind. If God offers Himself to us, and we don't come to Him, He just waits patiently for us. So why doesn't mankind give each other the same consideration? Seems to me there are too many people on Earth playing God. God will be waiting for those people when they die, and will judge them based on what they did to take His power from Him.

Now, where do you think the ideas to do that sort of thing come from? Yes, Satan! So this book is to open your eyes to what the prince of darkness is and has been doing to us since the beginning of mankind. It is to tell you that God is fed up with Satan harming His children, and has decided to end Satan's reign on Earth. But if we, His children, don't show God that we are willing to fight for our own lives against Satan, then God will not fight for us either.

Instead He will simply take the Angels and leave us to Satan and turn His back on us, the way we turn our back on Him and His love. And once the Earth has suffered untold horrors, then we get to go to hell and suffer for eternity. This is happening now, not in the future. God is calling us, this generation, to fight along side of Him, against Satan. This is the hard truth. This is the honest result of turning your back on God at this time in human history. There is no time for debate, no time for spending years trying to decide whether the world can believe if I was really listening to God. And God will prove that point to you in His time.

There is not one word in this book that will tell you to do anything but love God and follow His laws, and give God your life. So if you find yourselves opposed to what this book is saying to you, you have to ask yourself why you are questioning these facts. What do you have to lose? What are you holding onto that will not get you to Heaven? What are you doing that will only benefit you, while you are on Earth? What are you doing (honestly) for your fellow man? What are you doing for your soul, or is your body your only concern? What have you done for God or is what God can do for you, your only concern?

If you don't think I am hearing God, what spirit are you listening to? If your spirit is telling you anything negative, then I can assure you it is not God. As you read the words from the Angels and the words from God, you see that even the hardest lessons are said with a positive attitude and with kindness and love for mankind. If your spirit is telling you to think negative about mankind, either as a group or one person, it is not God. God does not tell anyone to kill, or harm anyone, in any way; physically or verbally. God only presents the truth and allows us to accept it or refuse it. So this plan is for you to accept or refuse, according to your own freewill. I am only allowed to present God's words in this plan to the world.

—God—received as this book was being written
"I give all truth forward regarding My plan of future's child. My thoughts of you run cold, when I am in so little prayer regarding your life with day of day survival. I give you glow with swift movement toward our plight, when is asked with prayer toward My mercy of you."

God will quickly give you His light when you ask His mercy daily. In His light, you will have knowledge to do all you need to do. If you don't ask, God doesn't spend much time thinking about your problems, as He said His thoughts run cold of you.

—God—continued

"If you choose course of one who after bring you toward his soul, will crush your life out under his footsteps (Satan), you will perish My home. Once Earth has brought Satan word that God's love is their blessing; then all Earth will flourish with abundance. All men will give hope, with flowers in hand, that counts with children toward loving wives. (Many will find love, marriage and children.) Many factories that once ended will come back again; people without lives glowing have reason once more for rejoice. (People who have been out of work will find jobs, because everything will change when we no longer are under the repression of Satan.) Never in history of Earth, has there been abundance like this that will give as Earth sees my truth for them, as increase with love makes everything new for the children. Many great events of this making will bless us against all evil forward. Man will be able to give hope and pray honest words towards God for making life wondrous more again. This promise is yours from His Most Honored Highness of all."

> God is promising us that if we live by His plan; all Earth will flourish as never before. Many great things will happen that will protect us against any evil from that time forward, until the end of the world comes of His will.

—God—continued

"I beg you see your end with pains remorse with Satan's evil astride; giving his venom and sickening your life, until you live pained with fear against God's laws for good. This will end lives of hell thus.

"Think strong towards this evil ones making Earth die plan; for his end will cut out lives of any who follow your seed. I say only of their sake, see evil as wrong end of day; he wills only destruction when he gives wealth, lust desire, great gifts of glitter, and hope no more."

> Honestly, I don't know what more God could say to us after He has promised us abundance on Earth and Heaven after we die. Satan only offers short time pleasures and has our destruction in mind when he is offering those earthly pleasures that he has planned to take from us as quickly as he gives them. Let me just remind you; if what you do is sinful or what you do causes someone else to sin, you are following Satan's plan to end Earth.

Hubert Van Eyck 1366-1426 Public Domain

39

Give Me Your Answer in Morning Glow of Day

—Angel—original words of the plan
"Give me your answer in morning glow of day; for then we will spend every moment then, in response to making us/you a healthy woman. Of this I can give promise; only if we take our course afoot towards God's end plan."

—Angel—translated
Give me your answer in morning glow of day, for then we will spend every moment in response to making you and any who read this, a healthy (fearless and strong) man or woman. I can promise this only if we take our course onward towards God's end of Satan's plan.

> The Angel was giving me a choice to accept this plan, to write this book and give my life to God for the sake of all on Earth. He gave me until morning the following day, but I answered immediately to devote my life to this plan. I was humbled greatly by this honor to serve God in a way that would allow me to help others, and I invite all of you to accept God's plan into your life and help as many others as you can.

Luke 14—**Jesus**
26 "If anyone comes to me and does not hate his father and mother, his wife and children, his brothers and sisters—yes, even his own life—he cannot be my disciple. 27 And anyone who does not carry his cross and follow me cannot be my disciple.

33 In the same way, any of you who does not give up everything he has cannot be my disciple. **"He, who has ears to hear, let him hear."**

40

This Book Begins Our Way to Save Earth

—Angel—original words of the plan
"So this is our schedule of truths.
One, this book will begin our way to give all who read it and more; Our LORD's
plan for keeping Earth safe from his morbid ways. Future times depend on you;
for this plan gives them courage/strength to fight His way."

—Angel—translated
One, this book will begin Our way to give all who read it and more; Our LORD's
Plan for keeping Earth safe from Satan's morbid ways. Future times depend on
you; for this plan gives them courage and strength to fight God's way.

—God—received as this book was being written
"All have known many who end their lives with no plan. They feel that whatever
happens on Earth is done because God is ruler over them. But you can see that
God will not give His blessed way of any who don't ask what be His will for
them; so evil source has deceived much about man and God upon Earth. No one
knows how God planned their lives out of love, because Satan kept you blind of
Us above with thoughts of more upon His Earth. Love of self when here; makes
only Satan happy."

> This you must know, many people on Earth live their life believing that
> whatever happens in life is God's will. This is not true. God only gives
> His will to those who give Him their freewill and ask for His will for
> them. That is the cold, hard truth that Satan has kept from you. God
> planned your life when you were created. So you should know that God
> planned a great life for you. If you are not living a great life *in every*
> *way*, then it is because you never asked God what His plan for you was.
> So you are living the life Satan has influenced, to make Satan happy.
> Satan has kept you blind to how to live a good and happy life.

41

I Have Been Waiting a Long Time for You

—Angel—original words of the plan
"Let's begin by saying that I have been waiting a long time for you to be willing/able to find courage/strength of spirit well; for our course from hell's glorified murder to soul's plan."

—Angel—translated
Let's begin by saying that I have been waiting a long time for you to be willing and able to find courage and strength of spirit well enough for our course from hell's glorified murderer of soul's plan.

> I guess God knew long before I did, that I would be willing to do this work in His honor. But I guess He had to wait for me to find the courage to accept this work

—God—received as this book was being written
"God has your life in mind when you are created. His will of your purpose has been well established, from conception until death. Each day of your life is His plan for your being on Earth. LORD God knows when you are created that your course will bring you all needed learning thus, to finish your plan with His will of you. Never think you have or serve other purpose alone of God, all is with His way. That is why it is important that We remind Earth that God is over all reason for life. God has given Our daughter more strength now, to give world courage needed against evil around all of Earth. Give all His words, for in you, We see continued effort until this evil ends."

> We are presented with opportunities to learn the things we will need to fulfill God's plan for our life. God hopes that somewhere along the way we actually ask Him what that plan is, but in the meantime, He does allow us to learn the things we will need when we finally open our mind to the thought that we have to give up our pride and our

selfish will of ourselves, and ask God what He wills us to do. God will simply wait for us.

You have to keep reminding yourself that it was God who created you, not simply your parents. So it's not your parents' plan for your life that is important, it is God's plan that you must find out. And your parents should be guiding you toward God for that information, instead of insisting that you follow in their footsteps.

You see how Satan can twist truth so that people see only self-indulgence? We even ignore the needs of our children to find God's plan, in order to satisfy our own pride of self; but all the while we tell ourselves it is for the good of our children.

The outcome is that children rebel against your will of them, and Satan just loves that outcome. He has made you argue, and made your children disrespect you, and caused your children to take some wrong roads to buck your authority over them. Some harm others because they have a need to show power, because their parents impose their own will on them, etc.

When Satan starts a ball rolling, it causes untold horror and conflict in our lives. It becomes one problem after another, to Satan's delight. When I asked for God's will, I had no idea that this book and spending the next twelve years of my life helping others to realize what God wants them to know about the truth of life was going to be God's will for me. But with His will, God has given me strength and courage to complete the work He wants me to do. God has also promised me a means to get this book out to the world. At this time in writing this book, I have no idea how I am going to afford to have this book published. But God has it planned, so I am listening to His words everyday with much enjoyment and awe, and writing each word with the trust that God will provide everything needed.

42

Divine God Is Calling You Today

—Angel—original words of the plan
"Divine God is calling you today, this time of history of life, for His purpose of letting everyone know this source of power exists around you/us; for the sole effort involved in bringing our world/Earth over to Heaven's enemy door hold/hell."

—Angel—translated
Divine God is calling you today, this time of history of life, for His purpose of letting everyone know, this source of power (Lucifer and his fallen angels) exists around you for the sole effort involved in bringing our world over to Heaven's enemy door hold of hell.

—God—received as this book was being written
"It is Our LORD's Divine order of you child (me); that you spend your time alone in silence, while listening to His words about Lucifer's course in action. In you God has given courage of placing His thoughts around the heads of great one's minds, to say that evil is not a myth, given to make you obey His laws; instead this source will end life and all should know Satan's efforts are doubling. They are increasing to take Earth's beings hell bound before God comes of Earth and brings all to Heaven. Time is running short for he (Satan) who knows God's end will not bring honor toward his way, and put his soul away from all who glorify God. Earth will end by God's hand when evil dwells below only. This will increase evil's hatred with Earth's beings, because they give God their lives again with love for only He. All evil will increase while God makes His effort of saving us from his (Satan's) evil ways."

> God is telling you that Satan will increase his efforts during the time God is fighting this battle with him; so think hard before you do something that causes harm to anyone, and think about how you are getting the ideas you get. Are your thoughts about love for your fellow man and how to help, or are they self-involved and only produce

happiness in your own life. Think about what you are selling, watching, doing, and make sure God would approve of them, because Satan is very good at convincing you that what you are thinking is justified; because you have the right of freewill, to choose what kind of life you want to live. Satan will not get you anything good after you make a wrong choice in this life; if you follow his thinking now, you also have to follow him into hell.

—God—continued

"Make this noted, you are all gravely warned that your life will perish with no reward of God, should you choose Satan before moving toward God's loving answer to save your lives now. Give His LORD only thoughts with good; for His great protection of your Earth is at hand."

Again you are being warned not to side with Satan, and to think about everything you are doing very carefully to see who it would benefit; God or Satan. You know God is only interested in love of each other, so if what you are about to do is not to show love for the person you are planning to do something to or with; then guess who is behind your plan, and watch what kind of horror unfolds if you proceed.

—God—continued

"I have made no point of keeping any part of this evil's plan from your minds. All must know what faces his future to avoid its happening. I praise My loved child Carol in her effort of bringing everything given her, for she has given Us her comfort of life, to say of Our end plan. But more will be made of her afore life comes end. Patient little girl of God, she will never be."

Well I guess God knows me pretty well! And it looks like this book is not God's only purpose for me in this life.

Psalm 139—For the director of music. Of David. A psalm.

1 O LORD, you have searched me
and you know me.

2 You know when I sit and when I rise;
you perceive my thoughts from afar.

3 You discern my going out and my lying down;
you are familiar with all my ways.

4 Before a word is on my tongue
you know it completely, O LORD.

5 You hem me in—behind and before;
you have laid your hand upon me.

6 Such knowledge is too wonderful for me,
too lofty for me to attain.

7 Where can I go from your Spirit?
Where can I flee from your presence?

8 If I go up to the heavens, you are there;
if I make my bed in the depths, you are there.

9 If I rise on the wings of the dawn,
if I settle on the far side of the sea,

10 even there your hand will guide me,
your right hand will hold me fast.

Prayer for No One Special

I pray Thee LORD for no one special,
For all is blessed of Thee.
For only God knows who is worthy
Of so much He today.

I pray Thee God so more will follow
In way of Yours today,
That only God is in their thoughts,
And on their lips, so full of heart I say.

So maybe once before I die,
I may deserve Your grace.
For pray of all mans, no one special,
And then all may be blessed.

I give You praise Almighty LORD,
For only He is God to souls;
Who struggle away from me no more,
But find a home blessed near to Thee.

Revenge is more of God's Earth beings,
Who stray toward hell's bemare,
But honest fear His lonely way,
For only God can hear.

Our calls for help away for He,
That harms we more than he,
When others choose our long endure,
Of helpless company.

Be brave my souls, for God can see,
When others cast His word of thee and me.

43

Love of God, Over Peace on Earth

—Angel—original words of the plan
"From this time forward; love over peace will score holes of steel into his shirt so cold of stones thrown. Blessed will be any who devour his (Satan's) words of guilt of pain, towards self love."

—Angel—translated
From this time forward, love of God over peace on Earth will score holes of steel into Satan's shirt, so cold from throwing stones at God. Blessed will be any who devour Satan's words of guilt, of pain, towards loving yourself first.

—God—explanation of the above received as this book was being written
"From this moment of your history, until all life ends; Earth's children will bear all scares made of his evil self, upon them. But as you turn from him to love God, this will increase pressure on his plan against you, until it scores holes into it. Your love with Your Maker, will let evil know of how God will drive stakes through his evil soul, for harming His children. Now God tells you that He will bless any who stand up against Satan, when doubt erupts against you. Those who honor Satan's way will talk evil wishes on behalf of your effort to save life on Earth. God wishes you love yourself enough to make your life eternal with Him. Evil hates your will of God and will send all force against this effort, to punish Earth's beings for giving God love. God wants you to fight evil through love and will send many blessings for those who learn this plan."

> I don't know about the rest of you, but those last statements from God, gave me chills. Many things happened while writing this book that proved these statements from God. Once I began working with God, Satan hounded me day and night. During the day with temptation, and during the night in my dreams, until some nights I just prayed to God to protect me, so that I could sleep. There were many times when I fell into Satan's trap for me and I had to ask God to forgive me for

becoming selfish and prideful and expecting more than God was willing to give to me at that time, You see, for a sinner such as me, this plan takes some getting used to.

The important part is to think about how you feel when you fall into the devil's trap. Most of the time, I find I feel miserable for not trusting God to take care of me. Jesus told me to just come to Him and give Him a reason to forgive me. I would do that, and still found it hard to let go of a sense of control. We all want to feel we have control over what should happen in our lives. We daydream about our futures, thinking that if we imagine them vivid enough, we can make them happen and God will just do as we want. This is not so. God's plan is different than you may have thought; it certainly was for me.

Jesus told me, "Just let go." If you let go of your control (freewill) Jesus will be there to catch you, he won't let you fall. If you are like me, you may be learning this with a lot of pain, and may have to try it over and over before you feel comfortable with it. But as long as God sees you are trying and each time coming for forgiveness, and asking God to get the devil off your back, then you will be okay. God will bless all your efforts to show Satan you have more love for God than desires for what Satan can do for you.

—Carol—original line from the plan
I asked, "What exactly do you want people to do to keep evil away and the coming of David?"

44

First, Pray Together in Strength of Voice

—Angel—original words of the plan
"First, pray together in strength of voice to call Our LORD in force upon his might, sworn to abate with evil souls. Say Our LORD's Prayer together for strength and wholeness against David."

—Angel—translated
First, pray together in strength of voices, to call Our LORD in force upon Satan's might, sworn to put and end to Earth with his evil souls. **Say Our LORD's Prayer together** for strength and wholeness against David.

> Pray daily, I know not everyone can go to church everyday, so I suggest to you to pray on the hour. Our LORD wants strength of voices, so with the time zones around the world, there should always be a group of people praying that God's plan will be successful for all of us.
>
> You need to say "The LORD's Prayer" in the morning when you get up. This one is just between you and God. It will be when you offer Him your freewill that day. It's good to do this everyday, because you really do need to remind yourself every day that you want God's will for you. It is in the words of the prayer you are saying. **"Thy will be done on Earth, as it is in Heaven."** And also, **"Give us this day our daily bread."** This line asks Our LORD to provide all you will need to live a good life and be able to fight evil.
>
> Then say "The LORD's Prayer" a second time, to ask God to fight Satan and put an end to his reign on Earth. **"And deliver us from evil."** Remember you are praying so that David will not be allowed to come and destroy Earth for your children and their children. Pray for this in the morning, in the afternoon and then once more in the evening before you thank God for all His efforts on your behalf that day.

Luke 11—**Jesus**

23 "He who is not with me is against me, and he who does not gather with me, scatters.

28 "Blessed rather are those who hear the word of God and obey it."

—God—received as this book was being written

"I ask My children on Earth of God, to call Me when evil dwells nearby you. Ask Me for guidance for I have all love answers for you. No other of Earth can protect against evil dwellers thus. Also give Me, each of you, a sign with love that My blessing comes into your life willingly from you. This alone can change Our plan of Earth because one indication that you care about who rules life is more hope of all others. Then all follow your guidance."

Call God when you know you are being tempted. Believe me, He is right there to help you. Just say to God, Please cast this evil devil away from me. Make sure God knows you are asking for Him willingly. Say the words, "**God, I will you to bless me with your protection against evil.**" This not only calls God's blessing to you, but Satan hears you as well and he will know you want God before him. I know it may not be the most popular thing to do right now on Earth; to call God for help out loud, but one day if more of us are calling God than are listening to Satan, it will be a welcome plea to hear.

If you hear someone around you asking God to help, pray with them because if Satan is close enough for them to be calling for help, he is close to you also, and God would want you to give this other person your love by helping him. You will become **a strength in voices against Satan**, which is exactly what God wants. Also if God casts evil from one person close to you, you may want to be praying so that the spirit doesn't take up residence in you.

(And keep praying)

Luke 11—**Jesus.** 24 "When an evil spirit comes out of a man, it goes through arid places seeking rest and does not find it. Then it says, 'I will return to the house I left.' 25 When it arrives, it finds the house swept clean and put in order. 26 Then it goes and takes seven other spirits more wicked than itself, and they go in and live there. And the final condition of that man is worse than the first."

45

Be Evermore Present in Church

—Angel—original words of the plan
"Be evermore present of His church; more so in evil morning or late turn noon, when justice dwells deep of hearts smite in gold rush hours. For this gold be thy answer for sins committed after greed strikes within hearts make weak of needs/wants."

—Angel—translated
Be even more present in church; go **in the morning when business begins** for the day or **late afternoon when it's the busiest part of a work day**. For this is when Satan puts thoughts in minds and hearts, that to make money, it is just to do it at all cost to those who will be hurt by your actions. For this gold is the answer for sins committed after greed strikes within hearts made weak of needs and wants.

Oh believe me, this is not just talking about those who are running businesses, or big business; this is also the little guy who can barely make ends meet. This is the lotto player and the gambler, the contest entry forms, the looter, the short-changer, the guy that takes a pen from the office cabinet. This is anyone, who because of his desires to be wealthy or pay his bills, finds a way to get there at someone else's expense, or falls into the devil's trap of getting money the easy way; or so we think, when the thought comes into our minds from Satan, who would love to see you sabotage your life.

Please see how the words of "Our LORD's Prayer" will drive holes into Satan's plan, and also ask God for his protection at all hours of the day. I know many churches have had to close during the day and some have closed their doors completely. But I have hopes that they will open again. In the meantime, if you can't pray at church, then pray at home or wherever you may be, while people all over the world are at work making decisions that will affect other people's lives. These poor souls will be face-to-face with Satan, so pray that they ask God for His will before making choices that are judged by God. Remember that God told us that when someone is in need, you are required to help them even if it is inconvenient.

(This includes praying for them.)

I call these Angels, **"The Wall Street Angels."**
Virchi_d Pietro Perugino 1450-1523 Public Domain

Luke 9—Jesus
The Parable of the Rich Fool

13 Someone in the crowd said to him, "Teacher, tell my brother to divide the inheritance with me."

14 Jesus replied, "Man, who appointed me a judge or an arbiter between you?" 15 Then he said to them, "Watch out! Be on your guard against all kinds of greed; a man's life does not consist in the abundance of his possessions."

16 And he told them this parable: "The ground of a certain rich man produced a good crop. 17 He thought to himself, 'What shall I do? I have no place to store my crops.'

18 "Then he said, 'This is what I'll do. I will tear down my barns and build bigger ones, and there I will store all my grain and my goods. 19 And I'll say to myself, "You have plenty of good things laid up for many years. Take life easy; eat, drink and be merry."'

20 "But God said to him, 'You fool! This very night your life will be demanded from you. Then who will get what you have prepared for yourself?'

21 "This is how it will be with anyone who stores up things for himself but is not rich toward God."

Do Not Worry—Jesus

22 Then Jesus said to his disciples: "Therefore I tell you, do not worry about your life, what you will eat; or about your body, what you will wear. 23 Life is more than food, and the body more than clothes. 24 Consider the ravens: They do not sow or reap, they have no storeroom or barn; yet God feeds them. And how much more valuable you are than birds! 25 Who of you by worrying can add a single hour to his life? 26 Since you cannot do this very little thing, why do you worry about the rest?

27 "Consider how the lilies grow. They do not labor or spin. Yet I tell you, not even Solomon in all his splendor was dressed like one of these. 28 If that is how God clothes the grass of the field, which is here today, and tomorrow is thrown into the fire, how much more will he clothe you, O you of little faith! 29 And do not set your heart on what you will eat or drink; do not worry about it. 30 For the pagan world runs after all such things, and your Father knows that you need them. 31 But seek his kingdom, and these things will be given to you as well.

32 "Do not be afraid, little flock, for your Father has been pleased to give you the kingdom. 33 Sell your possessions and give to the poor. Provide purses for yourselves that will not wear out, a treasure in Heaven that will not be exhausted, where no thief comes near and no moth destroys. 34 For where your treasure is, there your heart will be also.

Luke 16—**Jesus**

13 "No servant can serve two masters. Either he will hate the one and love the other, or he will be devoted to the one and despise the other. You cannot serve both God and Money."

46

Second, Smooth Flow Toward Justice Within Government

—Angel—original words of the plan
"Second, this plan requires smooth flow within souls, toward justice streaks within government. This means government agencies abridged with combat untie across grown countries in turmoil."

—God—explanation of the above received as this book was being written
"This refers only to **government agencies** that fight within the course of making laws of justice for Earth. These souls force others of Earth towards evil streaks of man, because they can't give what is right when trying to produce rules for their nations. So let us say that none with justice for his work can give the wrong choice with God and get away with it. For God sees his answers thus done, with hearts avenged in pain towards an end of peace. Now God has said His plan is a way for all of Earth to know, He will punish those who force mankind into a wrong way to live their lives.

No more will be said of this; for God has said His piece."

Well, this statement from God should put the fear of The LORD into every politician, lobbyist, judge, and military leader in the world. God is telling you that He knows what is in your hearts when you are voting on laws that cause other people to live the wrong kind of life.

So now you know that getting re-elected by God at the end of your life is going to depend on what you did in your job, and He doesn't intend to let you get away with anything. This might be a good time to look over some of the laws you hid some less desirable elements in, to satisfy someone funding your campaign, etc.; and rewrite those before God rewrites your ending.

I would also think a lot longer before going into war, allowing a drug that you know could harm or kill someone, increasing taxes, getting rid of programs for the elderly, or poor, etc. God is watching, and is telling the rest of us to watch with him. In other words, don't be so eager to vote for someone who is getting you into war; God tells us that war is the Devil's work. God's work is love for each other, do for each other, and don't harm each other. God wants all of us to start paying a lot closer attention to what our governments are getting us into. And is assuring those in government who think they can hide what they do from us, that they can't hide from God.

Keep in mind that the closer your relationship with God, the easier it will be to spot wrongs being done. Every last one of us will be able to get images from God that will point us in the right direction, and point us away from those who are trying to harm us.

Luke 11—Jesus
42 "Woe to you Pharisees, because you give God a tenth of your mint, rue and all other kinds of garden herbs, but you neglect justice and the love of God. You should have practiced the latter without leaving the former undone.

43 "Woe to you Pharisees, because you love the most important seats in the synagogues and greetings in the marketplaces.

44 "Woe to you, because you are like unmarked graves, which men walk over without knowing it."

45 One of the experts in the law answered him, "Teacher, when you say these things, you insult us also."

46 Jesus replied, "And you experts in the law, woe to you, because you load people down with burdens they can hardly carry, and you yourselves will not lift one finger to help them.

47 "Woe to you, because you build tombs for the prophets, and it was your forefathers who killed them. 48 So you testify that you approve of what your forefathers did; they killed the prophets, and you build their tombs. 49 Because of this, God in his wisdom said, 'I will send them prophets and apostles, some of whom they will kill and others they will persecute.' 50 Therefore this generation will be held responsible for the blood of all the prophets that has been shed since

the beginning of the world, 51 from the blood of Abel to the blood of Zechariah, who was killed between the altar and the sanctuary. Yes, I tell you, this generation will be held responsible for it all.

52 "Woe to you experts in the law, because you have taken away the key to knowledge. You yourselves have not entered, and you have hindered those who were entering."

47

Watch Waste Movement Grow Weaker

—Angel—original words of the plan
"Watch every waste movement grow weaker in thy scrutiny of its self involvement thus. Tread oh/only slow to peak thy nerves endings, after survive more strife afore it's more over. Send many into/for grief/woe before many can/will end all enemies thus."

—God—explanation of the above received as this book was being written
"This refers only of laws for justice changed of now. For when others take up God's cause to change plans made in government thus far; then all can see how watching our ruler's trade with other nations will give all errors with judgments made within laws created before this time. So don't let anything go without you seeing how God's plan can change our hearts, for any law towards God's good to the needs of all mankind. So this is, **'Scrutiny with Justice Based'**. Only of God will this be handled."

> God does expect the current laws on the books to be changed if they don't reflect the way God wants us to live. He is also watching the way we treat people of other nations in our trades with them. God says that if the laws were not made with good judgment and fairness for each side, it will show up as we trade.
>
> God wants all of us to scrutinize our laws and trades to make sure they are good for all mankind. God doesn't think any of us should be making trades without His influence. You see this is an area that Satan has especially been involved in.

—Angel—original words of the plan
—Second listing for additional explanation by God
"Tread oh/only slow to peak thy nerves endings, after survive more strife afore it's more over."

—God—continued

"The last sentence means this: When all of Earth have made the changes to create God's rules for justice, then some can still cause harm; so care should be made of this before all is sent on for God to judge thus."

> The other thought here is that some people will not choose to accept God's plan, so even if the laws change, some hearts will not. Satan will still have influence over some. We will need God to fight Satan on our behalf when this happens. Please keep in mind at all times that Satan is not going to back down. He is going to be fighting us every moment.

—God—continued

"I will say only; give My laws first consideration over mankind laws. No law from God is wrongdoing. I have given only just cause of My way, no time of history have I given even one man cause of change this."

Matthew 4—Jesus

7 "It is also written, 'You shall not put the LORD your God to the test.'"

> God has a few things to say about us changing His laws to suit our lifestyles and our selfish desires. He is not very happy that over all these years many people have put pressure on the churches to accommodate the masses who feel their priorities are more important than God's priorities, and their ideas of what is right and wrong are more correct than God's idea of what is the correct way to live in order to be worthy of Heaven.

> Some of the changes God gives in this book are going to be very hard for many people to accept. However, mankind has not changed since Adam and Eve; the Earth has not changed since God created it. The only thing that did change is our perception of what we think is important and how we are seeing the delusion God Has created for our view.

> We seem to think for some reason that way back when God created these laws and gave them to Moses, that those people were supposed to obey them, but over the years the laws have become obsolete for today's life. God, however, sees you the same way he saw Moses. You look the same, talk the same, walk the same, have the same desires, the same urges, etc. and you live on the same Earth he created billions of years ago.

So why would the laws that the perfect God who knows all (even into the future, our time) need to change to satisfy you. God seems to think He is right, and always was right. God seems to think we have made some mistakes along the way, and changed laws He created to accommodate our selfish desires. Furthermore, God thinks that Satan is behind those changes and our attitudes that we are more important than what God wants. God said if you want to find truth, you can find it through abilities from Him.

—God—continued

"Now more of man has caused Our way wrong information given (Over the years man has given wrong information about the laws of God.) and this I am about to change through Our daughters praise of Us, through Our book. I see many church has made adjustments of My truth. I will adjust these again for them. This time you will see fit of them, for nowhere is it written that God has ignored all made form agreements with man."

God has not ignored any agreements He has made with mankind through covenants or commandments.

. . . .

—God—continued

"I have given laws regarding life but Earth man has adjusted My cause of life. I tell you now that if one interferes one moment of time upon another's life force; he will give Me just cause when condemning his soul at the end of his very own life."

Pulling the plug, giving others drugs, slayings, drunk driving, wars, fights between two people, creating bombs, etc. and anything that causes another man's life to end.

. . . .

—God—continued

"I have said no fellow upon God's Earth is favored against his fellow man for sexual pleasure (same sex relationships); this I have no means of changing. All Earth is favored only with opposite attraction soul. I give only this law; forbid all else. I will give fair judgment in these people. No man lives alone, for they are in My eyes. There is no course of action that I will accept in this."

God does not approve of same-sex, intimate relationships. Sex is supposed to be only between a man and a woman, no exceptions. The idea that you were born with the desire for the same-sex, came from Satan, and you may feel that God created you that way, but He did not. God created you the way He wanted you to be, to live with the laws He also created. Satan can easily change the thoughts of children who are not on Earth long enough to understand what Satan has done to them. That is why it is very important for parents to protect their children from this kind of thinking. Be sure to pray for God to protect your child from all the evil influences that Satan can impose on them. Start telling your children when they are young, what consists of a family in the eyes of God.

Those of you who have been living this lifestyle will have to make some very hard choices now as will the rest of us who fit the other categories of law-breakers listed here. None of us are going to find it easy to live this plan. I am sure there will be many who will want to put the plan down and condemn me for bringing this book to your knowledge. After all, doing the right thing is not the easy thing; and we want the easy way and the way we have gotten used to. We don't want change, not even if it means losing our souls and losing our Earth. We are the generation that feels we should be able to do whatever we please, and so we simply rewrite any laws that don't suit our purpose. We call these loopholes, but God calls it like it really is. Truth from the one being that sees everything, visible and invisible.

May I say one thing more about this? God really doesn't care what your government allows you to do, or how many times you insist on your equal rights. This book is what God is saying today, this time in history, to you and me. You have freewill to choose the fallacy you live with now, or the truth you should be living with. We are required through this message to change all the laws we on Earth created to favor our will over God's will for us.

. . . .

—God—continued
"I see God is not allowed of children where class is given. (Prayer in schools) Our sign is needed of them who are learning how to properly give of each other. This in some nations will give Us cause for give correction."

God wants prayer in schools. If it is a problem to pray the traditional prayers because of all the different religions of children in school, then why not write a new prayer that will enable these children to call upon God's will for them, so that they can benefit by His divine knowledge? We don't want children to do it the hard way, if they can unite with God and learn so much easier.

Here is a prayer God gave me, and I think this little prayer should not offend any religion. It offers our freewill to God and asks for His will for our day.

> **"Almighty God,**
> **I will Thee give Your knowledge,**
> **so that answers come suddenly;**
> **for knowing Thy will,**
> **can enable the right course of this day."**

If you are an atheist, I can assure you there is a God, and He will welcome you back to Him. To God you are the lost sheep, and the one He goes looking for. All Heaven will rejoice at your safe return home. But I warn you that Our LORD will not give you Heaven unless you come to Him. That is the one huge stipulation and the one thing God feels the worst about. Nothing hurts God more than one of His Children turning away from Him. You may be the nicest person on Earth, but if you don't go to God, all will be lost for you when you die.

· ·

—God—continued

"I have come upon many who bring every problem of church out in public domain. I say don't send man cause with torch burning of them; Our laws with God separate with land law."

If your concern is about God and church, it should be handled within the church. If your concern is about government or property it should be handled by government.

Don't send man into the public with a burning issue of religion. God is referring to holy wars, abortion, pulling the plug, etc. If God gave a law, He expects that law to remain intact and not dissected and pulled apart to accommodate all the different religions and races and sexes.

And that is what happens when you take God's laws before the government and courts. Suddenly one or more groups of people who don't want to obey the law the way God laid it out decide that it is against their rights as citizens and God's law should be changed to satisfy them. God's answer to you is simply that you are wrong, and God is right.

Let me remind all of you again, this Earth belongs to God alone. All laws must, must, must reflect His way. We have no rights over God. We have no rights over each other. We are all equal to God. This Earth was for all of us to live our lives in peace. Not for us to fight over trivial issues that truthfully won't make one bit of difference once we die.

Let's make this clear, if we are all doing God's will, then we should have no reason to argue over the way a law is written or upheld. God is not going to tell one person one thing and another something different so that He doesn't offend anyone. For God, the concern is more whether you are offending Him, since He has all the power and you have none. He is holding your life in His hands and your afterlife as well.

Do you really want to offend Him with your selfish desires or your petty little arguments over the tiny bit of power you may think you have acquired on Earth? Really, think hard about who you are trying to fool. Do you think any amount of power you have on Earth compares with the power of God? You are an extremely small fish in a huge ocean. I can't begin to tell you how tiny your existence is, and how humble you should be instead of walking around proud and full of demands over what you want. If you knew God, you would be asking, "What do you want, God. I am your servant." You would change your prayers immediately the way I did, in the presence of God.

Please let me tell each and every one of you this fact. God is united with each of us. When someone is looking at you, it is God. When someone is asking for your help, it is God. When you kill someone, it is God. When you cheat someone, it is God. When you go to war with someone, you are fighting God. There is nothing, not a plant, animal, person, planet that is not God. So what do you think you can do to anything or anyone and not offend God?

—God—continued
"Give of Us then give them also. Government of people will think evil of Us if they are allowed course with help people live prayerful end."

Governments may choose a course of action that does not come from
God, to end a problem that concerns only church and God.

. . . .

—God—continued
"I will see end toward justice of future life souls that count nothing less of
Earth."

God wants an end to Governments making laws that allow the right
to choose abortion.

—God—continued
"All life, given of Us, starts when God says. Man will make no further assessment
thus. Cancel any laws of this regard immediately. No end will come to any of
God who have birth forming within. All of life be important for them no matter
what each circumstance has encased it."

No matter what the circumstance, no life is to be ended because all
life is important. By the way, God told me that a soul is given to a
child at conception, so there is never a time to abort, when you are
not taken a life. If conception happens, then it is God's choosing for
this to happen.

> **—God—June 15, 2006**
> **"This I say, no child of God has been without soul.**
> **Soul gives life and life gives man"**

. . . .

—God—continued
"All graves given thus will remain given."

This is in regard to digging up graves of anyone, no matter how long
ago they were buried.

—God—continued
"No man with Earth, legally or morally, is of right to strip these souls their resting
place. I will raise all souls upon Earth, on the final day. Any who have been sent
away have been brutalized of this event thus. I will punish heavily, any who cast
doubt over our dead corpus members enough to raise each above the soil they
have selected for their burial ground.

God will punish anyone who is just curious about these people enough to bring them out of their graves.

—God—continued

"Many great leaders rest upon soil disturbed for wealth sake. Many say for history proof, but God sees its true value of them, who protect its evidence raised forth."

> If you are digging up graves for wealth and saying it is for historic proof, God sees what you are doing to protect the evidence you bring out of the grave.

• •

—God—continued

"All things legal are not favorable with God. It is not favorable to consume drugs with narcotic base, for evil spirits are able then to enter souls low in force of will. This will cause many harm when healed with these demons still attached of them."

> If you are taking drugs that lower your will power, evil spirits will enter your body, because you will not realize what is happening and they will stay with you.

—God—continued

"Also, can't give Our favor around smoke of these weeds (Tobacco and Marijuana). All is making human blood go bad when breathe within form."

• •

—God—continued

"I have not agreed with Our laws based of hard-core sexual novels written of men who give courage to others of this sorted end. Now I say this, any who handle each in this way, will end his life lying alone of all source given man."

> This includes, books, magazines, movies, internet, etc.; if what you write is encouraging another to do something sexually against God's laws; God will take all source of sexual pleasure from you and you will end your life lying alone in that manner.

—God—continued

"I see what is going around my Earth of internet sort of pleasure. My will in this gives all who attract these around their life, grave remorse of Our course for you."

Well again, God is cautioning you to use the internet for good purposes and not evil ones. You may think no one sees you, but God sees everything, and He is the one being you do not want to cross actions with; especially now that He has laid down the law for this fight with Satan.

· ·

—God—continued

"No man is of his own accord, this of Us is important to see. I will never allow one man pleasure over another with targeted base given, that will destroy innocent people as a side-happening event. My Earth glows with life given by My hand, no other than by My hand is life taken. Give your enemy his end, will give your end up as well at the hand of God."

We are all here for only God's purpose of us; so then, no one is allowed to end the life of an innocent person as a means of punishment, for the sins of another. God is the only one allowed to judge if a life is to be taken and the only one allowed to take that life from this Earth. If you end a life, you end your life as well at the hand of God.

This is in regard to war, courts, personal battles with others, etc. All end of life is considered in this statement. If end of life is at your hand and/or your command of it, in any way, you are ending your own life with God at that moment. There are no exceptions. You have no right to justify someone else's end of life. This also includes Holy wars and religious wars of any sort. Unless you are personally given God's words (like in the Bible) to go to war or battle, you are not permitted to take a life. (God told us earlier in this book that He has not asked anyone to go to war since before the birth of Christ.)

I will say to you, don't be fooled by the Devil, God does not issue negative orders. If what you think you hear from God is a negative command, pray harder and ask God to send Satan away from you. Keep praying until you get an answer that sounds like the kindness of Our LORD.

· ·

—God—continued

"If a man has killed against your friend or family, you can try him in court, and he is to be killed if found guilty with no doubt. But should he be held against will of course (unjustly held and accused) then you will free him with proper atonement of your actions, by providing him justly all money lost of he and any evidence destroyed regarding his accusations. Publicly freed for all to see."

> There is to be no record left in anyone's files regarding this innocent man. No one should be able to judge him once he is found innocent. If you bring someone up on charges you better be prepared to restore his life completely if he is found innocent.

· ·

—God—continued

"I say this in regard to flogging another; I regard this act as violence taken under sinful cause. Should you give hand or fist or chain of your will against one who has unjustly offended you; you will disregard My will. Of this course in action I am the only one you will offend. I have said of you, that you must offer your attacker your other cheek to strike, before you lift one hand in your defense of the same manner that you received. For I am his master being, the one who judges his actions toward others. I am the one who will offer this servant My justice strong against him for giving My son with Earth pain. Go away from him quickly as you can after he has offended, and I will present this soul his part of My plan for his judgment thus."

> God is telling you that if someone harms you verbally, physically, financially, etc.; do not take personal or on the spot action against him to get revenge or get even. Take what he is giving you and walk away from him quickly, because God sees what he is doing and will justify for you, what this man has done to you. But if you take action, you offend God by taking His power away, and using your will over His will for this man and you. You will suffer twice, if you choose your will over God's will of you; once at the hand of man and once at the hand of God. You might consider how much stronger God's justice is than anything you can do. Also you do not know what evil forces may be behind the actions of another. It is best to leave it to God to handle, because God knows exactly what the situation is.
>
> You then need to ask God what his will is regarding prosecuting under the law of government in cases regarding property or severe personal injury.

· ·

—God—continued

"I know my children dream of good honorable payment towards their labors, for this, I ask all who honor Me this time with Earth, to give of they who toil your work place, equal consideration when choosing amount you think appropriate of them. Do not judge based upon likeliness toward good humor of yourself or fast action within work force because of temperament. Give justly, regarding evidence given of their labors. All who qualify of equal labor, then qualify equally toward end expense of them. I see many who are laboring enough of two persons; who live poorly based of your end favor toward their labor; while others of your companies, wealth great in comforts overwhelming and unjustly caused. I will give these who end other's joys of Earth thusly, Our end of Heaven thusly. Many will see a reward for loss of Earth joys when end of their life brings them joys with Me."

> God is telling us that if we are not just to our workers and offer them the pay they deserve and their life suffers because of it, while others have an over-abundance that they do not deserve, because they were judged not by their work, but by their personality or because they are brown-nosing; then we will be judged by God in regard to what we did. Many of the ones who suffer at your hand will see Heaven, the ones who make them suffer will not. Always check the output of individuals work done of their own ambitions, not what someone has delegated to others. It is your responsibility to God to know who is doing the work in your company, and pay them justly. The Big Boss is watching.

. . . .

—God—continued

"I say of living with our elders, give all parents or elder persons your respect. These souls are closer of God because they raise forth children that God has given for them. All work done toward Our LORD's will is Godly love and will be given many rewards of Us who have asked of it. Should any give elders cause of evil strife, lonely evenings, or long forlorn of safety, then We will see to it that they live a long time, giving them many earthly events to change their end with hazards and strife. Alone or in bed against their want, they will say regrets for eternal end of life will give many problems."

> Be kind to elder persons or your end will be filled with hazards and strife. You will find yourselves alone in bed praying for an end to come because life will be so much less than you want it to be.

For those of you who are making laws regarding care for the elderly, either income or medical care or housing, please take heed of what God is saying to you. This message is not just for children who should be available to their parent; it is for anyone who God feels is responsible for a situation these people find themselves in. Keep in mind that no matter how much money you have, if you are doing anything to harm the elderly, God will find a way to make sure you experience exactly what you will deserve. I have to add here, God does not give problems to you, but on the other hand, if you are not doing His will, why should He take your problems away? *God is just,* and will treat you *just as* you treat others.

· ·

—God—continued

"Give my love of all who pray daily for souls in Purgatory/hell, for they are My lost ones who I still honor of love; for only through prayer of you, can My souls be redeemed of this place. My child is of your life, who I give freedom to hear their lonely cries of you, who wish give Me your prayer. I tell you this of Us; be of special regard, for no other way is Earth able of unconditional love toward fellow man, than to give others your effort of redemption this way. I have said, My blessing will come of all who pray of this end. Any of they who come for another's cause will see Me upon his own death."

> I have heard some people say that there is no Purgatory, but this is wrong. Our LORD allowed me to hear the souls in Purgatory crying out for prayers. The day it happened to me, it was completely unexpected and frightened me to death. But I came out of it knowing the importance of praying for those who are not allowed to pray for themselves and also it gave me great reason to change my life, so that I would not end up there.

Matthew 6—**Jesus**
Giving to the Needy

1 "Be careful not to do your 'acts of righteousness' before men, to be seen by them. If you do, you will have no reward from your Father in heaven.

2 "So when you give to the needy, do not announce it with trumpets, as the hypocrites do in the synagogues and on the streets, to be honored by men. I tell you the truth; they have received their reward in full. 3 But when you give to the needy, do not let your left hand know what your right hand is doing, 4 so that your giving may be in secret. Then your Father, who sees what is done in secret, will reward you.

5 "And when you pray, do not be like the hypocrites, for they love to pray standing in the synagogues and on the street corners to be seen by men. I tell you the truth; they have received their reward in full. 6 But when you pray, go into your room, close the door and pray to your Father, who is unseen. Then your Father, who sees what is done in secret, will reward you.

Photo by **Carol Aubuchon**
Assumption Grotto, Detroit, MI.

This is where my experience took place. This little Grotto is in the back of a cemetery, behind Assumption Grotto Church. I had gone there many times as a child, on the feast of Our Lady's Assumption, on August 15th. I remember hundreds of people crawling across the gravel path leading to this alter. But this day, my companion and I were the only two there. I found a Rosary on the alter, and I picked it up to say the prayers. I had only said a few prayers when I heard a voice tell me to lay face down on the marble step. I obeyed immediately, and that is when the visions and sounds came to me.

I was above them, looking down. I saw hands reaching up to me, trying to grab my attention. I heard thousands and thousands of voices crying and screaming. They were crying,

"Pray for me."
"Pray for me."
"Please, pray for me."

It was as if they knew I was there to help them and so they all tried to get my attention, one yelling louder than the next; saying the same thing, over and over again. ***"Please, pray for me."***

I was so frightened, that after only a few moments, I stood up and put the Rosary back on the alter, and grabbed my companion's arm, dragging her out of the cemetery as I told her about what happened.

When I asked God about this day, He told me I had to see this before He gave me His message for mankind. He wanted me to understand what I was fighting for. God showed me Purgatory so that I could give all of us a reason to go to His side for protection from Satan. I asked God to promise me that he would never show me hell. This was frightening enough.

I notice that in Purgatory, there is a lack of light, and everything seemed grey and dismal. But those who were crying to me had hope that mankind would help them. Please pray for these souls; some of them had no one on Earth that cared enough about them to keep them from sin, and no one now who thinks to pray for their souls. When you pray, ask God to give your prayers to souls He chooses, so that all who have been there a long time have a chance to go to Heaven.

We are asked by God to love our fellow man, but until you begin to pray in true unconditional love for those you know and don't know, who are on Earth and in Purgatory; you will not understand the meaning of **"Expanded Love"**. This is the type of love God has for all mankind. Most of us know a love between two persons, or love for your family and friends, but God wants us to love everyone, equally. He wants you to love your enemies; to do so will change your attitude toward them.

Here is how I look at people: We are made up of a human-side which goes through an awful lot on Earth; we have a freewill that makes us prideful and critical, and is subject to all the temptations Satan can throw at us each day. We also have a God-side; our soul that does no wrong, and is kind and gentle and loving of everyone. Our God-side is not subject to Satan at all, because it is protected by God as long as we do not turn our backs on Him.

We all fall into Satan's traps for us, whether small or large. These are hard to avoid in our situation. When someone does something to you that does not show love, then you must first realize where that is coming from. It does not come from the God-side, even though the God-side gets hurt by it. It comes from the human-side that was outsmarted by Satan. (Who by the way has the knowledge of Angels, and is invisible and so hard to detect by us.)

Do you think you should stand there and judge this person without knowing what Satan has done to them? No. For this reason, you must leave judgment up to God who knows everything. Do you think you can forgive this person, who has God within him? Well if you don't, you are not forgiving God, and then Satan wins. Not only does Satan win the cruel trick that he played on this person standing before you, but he also wins the trick he is playing on you.

Because now, you are standing up to God and saying, **"I don't forgive You, and I want to punish You for what You did."**

Wow! Does that make Satan happy. He just suckered two of God's children and walks away snubbing his nose at God, saying, **"You see . . . they listen to me because I am mightier than You."** Satan looks at us and says; **"I can make you do anything I want, you fools."**

Do you see now why God is giving us a plan to get rid of this evil around us? Unless we have God's knowledge and help, we are pretty much at Satan's beck and call. If he doesn't get you with one thing, he will get you with another. Satan never, ever stops.

God tells you in this plan that He is the only safe-haven, the only one who knows how to stop Satan. Let me just say this: If you think while you are reading this that you don't fall into his traps, then you have just committed the sin of pride and Satan is laughing at you right now. Not so easy to be perfect, is it? For this reason, it is very important to learn to forgive. Just learn to forgive the God-side and it will come a little easier. It is also important to pray for the souls in Purgatory, who fell into Satan's traps a few too many times for God to accept them into Heaven, where everything is pure and holy. Give those poor souls your unconditional love and get them to Heaven. If you pray with unconditional love enough, maybe God will forgive all the traps you have fallen into.

—Holy Spirit

"I say unto you, My Earth souls; My love for you has never changed in all this way of life. I give you all My will over death's enemy, to bring My many souls of Me. Tell of all souls thus forth, that Our child has brought Our way forth of you. In all ways she will bring Our heavenly course in action of those who without this help can justly end in Our enemies belong (hell). I with God have asked this soul of Ours who fears justly this end, to give her whole being upon the request of the Father, to save all Our Earth's members. I give her Our most honored gifts from his Almighty to present Our children on Earth by healing of them of any done of evil sources. I give ability for give many His power toward evil by adjusting minds toward His of God through many spiritual favors from Us. She will be about your Earth, giving love through make well and show power toward His Almighty with miracles form when of God has approved they. Our LORD is with her all days, from the very event given in prayer toward Him. Now he has given Our cause hers of this life."

> Okay. So doing God's will is way beyond what I imagined for my little life. I smile about this, when I am not shaking in my boots, and praying that I don't offend God by messing something up. I keep remembering Moses, and how he never got to see the promise land. God has spent some time convincing me that I am the servant and He is the Master. Whenever I fear being able to do His will, He finds a way to remind me who has the power and is the boss here.

> I can't tell you how many of God's rules I had to learn the hard way. I also can't tell you what God has in store for me much more than what you are reading here. I was told not to think about it, that when God wanted me to do something for someone, He would tell me on the spot. So for us, everyday is an adventure created by God. I can tell you that I am definitely beginning to understand the meanings behind, "Tremor in thy gut," and "Number in thy ear."

> The only thing I know for sure is that God wants me out and about, giving people courage to fight along with Him, through this plan. This is amazing to me, especially with all the physical and financial problems I have right now. So I am looking forward to seeing just how God intends to get me all over the world. He has assured me that He has this all planned out. God has made this my cause for life. God will help you to believe the power behind His plan with special blessings. I Have a feeling we will all get some wonderful blessings from God.

I want to share this statement from God that I got on 8-21-06, after learning another lesson from God.

—God

"God will only give as giving occurs in His account of your needs, never of your requirement knowledge; for God has full account; when you only see your own problems due you. I wish all to know, I give of this method to all who ask Me for help.

"Some feel I ignore their needs or am not allowing them the pleasures in life that others receive, but I do not play favoritism of any one; all are just as precious with Me. "I give of them only as far as I see they require for that day, to fulfill My desired purpose given to them by Me. Other than that, they should not ask more then I need of them. It is My desires that are important of this life; for they should know My end of their life comes with fulfillment with what I expect for them—not what they see of what should be so."

Matthew 10—Jesus
9 Do not take along any gold or silver or copper in your belts; 10 take no bag for the journey, or extra tunic, or sandals or a staff; for the worker is worth his keep. (You are a worker of God, when you are doing the will of God.)

I only want to give you a little more insight into this Bible passage. When you are giving your freewill to God, remember it is important to leave your baggage behind. If God gives you His will for your life and you are hanging on to the baggage you think you can't live without, you cannot give 100% of yourself to God's purpose for your Life. It is very difficult to just let go of everything you think is important in life, but it is the only way you will fulfill what God has in mind for you.

When I first read these words from Jesus, I thought as most of us did, that it was referring to clergy. It was said to the Apostles and so we would assume Jesus meant that they who leave their homes to give their life to the church, but Jesus was saying this to all of us. To follow Him who is God, you must leave everything else in order to free your mind enough to accept what God wants from you.

Don't get me wrong, God does not want parents to leave their children, He wants you to mentally leave everything that will keep you from hearing Him. He wants you to leave comfort and pleasures, as well as plans for the future. He may also want you to do something that means leaving your job or home, etc., but don't fear; He will make it possible in His way for you to do it. You should know that if you hold onto your life out of fear, you will lose what is most important.

Remember in the Bible, all the stories about the servants and the masters? Well, guess what Jesus was trying to get across to us?

We are the servants of the greatest Master of all. Even in your capacity as business owner, and boss over others, as well as parent, you are still the servant of your Master in Heaven, and still expected to act as the servant of man, and not the master. We are all here to serve as God requires us to serve; taking care of each other, instead of only expecting others to take care of us. There is only one Master, one who gives all orders; we are the servants.

—Angel—original words of the plan
—Second listing for additional explanation by God
"Send many into/for grief/woe before many can/will end all enemies thus."

—Angel—translated
This plan will send many people into grief, before many of us will end all enemies.

—God—explanation of the above received as this book was being written
"So many people will be sent for Satan's place in the pit of hell before others will bring governments around towards God's way plan for living upon his Earth."

> This is going to be a long battle with Satan. Unfortunately, Satan will take many souls to hell before those in power in Governments will come around to realizing they have to change their thinking. We need to do a lot of praying for our fellow man in positions that affect our living circumstances.

—God—received as this book was being written
"All will be asked, but many will refuse God because they will not see His message as a new proper form of life. They will stick to what has been shown them through the teachings of their churches. They will justify their cause to shun God's plan as one shuns all evidence given of this throughout the writings of the Bible. Many will not see who gives this cause of Earth to them. They will believe that if God willed this happen, some would be able to see these teachings among His past scripts. But in His book of then, many times it states that many have no eyes who read; many have not ears who listen and those who have this plan source knowledge will save Heaven for those who don't know of it themselves. I beg you see of this without eyes for souls need only know the truth within to hear God. God will appear of those; when with My daughter's ears and eyes you will get this knowledge given thusly."

> God tells us here that those of us who follow this plan will save the Earth for those who will never see or hear the truths given in the holy

books. Many will be so stubbornly determined to keep the teachings they know and respect and have come to rely on. They will not open their minds up to realize that God is not limited to the words in the holy books. God can change anything at anytime, and is doing that now.

To help those who think they have to stick to what they feel is the only answer, let me remind you that God, in His divine wisdom, flooded the Earth to rid it from the results of evil once before. He has also destroyed cities completely if He felt no good was left in them. This was done numerous times as stated in the holy book. Even God has a boiling point as to what He will tolerate from Satan. God has reached that point now, He has chosen to rid Earth of Satan because He has sorrow and love for us that have endured this evil for so long.

God can see that in all these years, we have not figured out how to live with His grace, to keep us from falling into Satan's traps. So one, He is telling us how to access His grace, and two, He promised us through a Covenant with Noah that He would never flood Earth again.

He wants us to prove once and for all to Satan that we choose God over his evil. Once we prove this to Satan, He will take Satan from Earth; if we fail to fight Satan along with God, He will let David come to Earth and the Earth will end the way it is written in the holy book. You should realize however, this is the only chance Earth is going to get. This book is how God is telling you this statement.

We are all the chosen people to fight Satan; the fight is now, and the consequences of ignoring this fight are so horrible that they are indescribable.

Sadly, there are still some who will not bend to the will of God, and for them, the end of anything good about life will be at their death.

> *God smiles at you for now you know,*
> *That life is more than powerful shows.*
>
> *You wear His label upon your face,*
> *When in disgrace you see His face.*
>
> *So look for Him after every trace of bad,*
> *For He is there, you will never be sad.*

48

Third, Our LORD Will Rise Out Above the Earth

—Angel—original words of the plan
*"Third, will be this hardest plea for justice cause. **Many will see Our LORD rise out above His Earth;** for He will send our team of Angels ahead should callus forms remain in front for you, only to be able to hide more evil attuned."*

—Angel—translated
Third, will be this hardest plea for the cause of justice. **Many will see Our LORD rise out above His Earth**; for He will send our team of Angels ahead of His coming, in case evil spirits try to hide your site of God, so that they can continue to do evil towards you.

> This is not something that will happen far into the future, but something that will happen fairly soon. God will give us time to accept the teachings of this book, and His Plan. Our God loves us and wants all His children to be with Him in Heaven and by His side, in this fight against Satan, therefore, He is willing to come to Earth to show you what you are up against. For this one time, Our LORD will come above the Earth for all to see. He will send Angels in advance, to make sure evil spirits do nothing to keep you from seeing Our LORD. Remember, as you are seeing The LORD, He is also seeing you. He will be here to show you what you are fighting for and who you are fighting against.

—God—received as this book was being written
"When God comes upon His Earth, nothing will be able to leave until He allows it to go. All evil will show around you, as this will give evidence of what God has given your life while under His protection. You will know His divine love before you are asked by His will toward your soul if you give all power over your love of Him or life with His way your whole effort. When you see truth is all around, you will gratefully give His Almighty your will of you. For then, all creation belongs in His way. God has given this end for Satan, to know His power

is strong against any who defy Him. Earth will survive only of God by the side of each soul bound toward His grace."

When God comes, He will let us see the evil around us before He asks us if we are ready to give our freewill up for His will of us. Seeing the truth will change any who have not come to God. He will do this to show Satan His power against any who defy Him. For those of you who are already giving God your freewill and asking His will for you, this day will confirm God's love for you, and the Angels will help you to bear the evil you will see. For those who refuse God, this day will scare the hell out of you, literally. It is God's intent to make sure you see what you are siding with, and how Satan and his evil souls will fear God.

This day is not Judgment day, but a day of commitment to a new form of life for all of us. No one who is on Earth this day will want to select Satan's path as a way of life. God wants your answer this day. When all on Earth choose God, then He will take Satan from Earth. This will not end Earth, but instead, it will begin a new way of living for us, with God as a close part of everyday life. *All things on Earth will change as of this day.*

—God—continued

"I give this as a sign that I will allow My souls time more upon My Earth, given in hope they can find Me in all they do from this day forth. All Earth will flourish thusly, until mankind gives God all his love forever as a way for Us to bring each soul back into Our Heavenly Palace.

I will protect you as I promised, My beloved man who entered Earth for My sake. You will receive every blessing of Us to live safely with loving ends. This of Us is given of all who justify Our plan against his evil force. Love of mankind makes this Our purpose for man."

God gave you this information so that you know that He has changed the game plan. There is no way our beloved God is going to let Satan harm His souls without a fight. God is giving us a new Earth after this battle with Satan, provided we all fight on His side, now. Earth will not be destroyed if we find God in every single thing we do from April 05, 2006, the day He gave this plan to me, until our end in Heaven. God is giving us more time on Earth because before we can go to Heaven, He wants to see us living this plan. Until we do, many of us are not worthy of Heaven, but from the day Our LORD comes to Earth forward, we will live safely from evil. We will learn to love each other and live the way God planned Earth when He created Adam and Eve. We will no longer have the influence of evil around us, and Earth will prepare us for the way it is in Heaven. We are here on Earth for God's sake, and as our loving Father, God wants us to know He will protect us when we ask it of Him.

I don't know how long God plans to keep Earth after He has made this change, but I do know that if we don't change, God does not plan on keeping Earth for much longer. You are being asked to save Earth. Not with weapons against a seen enemy, but with love against an unseen enemy, who hates us and hates God and hates love.

This unseen rival will fight back relentlessly the entire time, with weapons that cause you to desire money, in a greedy fashion, and inexplicably crave sexual pleasures that God forbids and finds deplorable. You will think it's enjoyable to torment others when these spirits inspire your minds with wicked thoughts. This torture of your senses will come with such an ungodly intensity that you have never experienced before in your life. This enemy will make you blind to righteousness, and twist your minds so badly that you will think you are doing well.

Always look at the way things are introduced to you. If you see God's love and are going to Him everyday to ask His will for your life, you will be safe. If you stay away from God and get a message in your mind that is negative and hateful, it is Satan. Pray hard for yourselves and others. You will have no idea from what direction Satan will attack you. He will always attack your most vulnerable spots. Examine your life; any area that is in need, Satan will come to fill that need.

***Psalm 37*—David**

27 Turn from evil and do good;
then you will dwell in the land forever.

28 For the LORD loves the just
and will not forsake his faithful ones.
They will be protected forever,
but the offspring of the wicked will be cut off;

29 the righteous will inherit the land
and dwell in it forever.

Gustave Dore 1833-1883 Public Domain

49

Never Let Out Your End

—Angel—original words of the plan
Never let out your end; thus courage spell end of you.

—God—explanation of the above received as this book was being written
"If you say nothing to God in your behalf, when you are facing death; your courage ends your life with God. This is not for everyone who faces death; it is only the few who give pleasure of self over pleasing God.

"All your life, give Us grace through your actions toward each other. Should your life end abruptly, you should give Heaven thought."

Luke 17—Jesus
33 Whoever tries to keep his life will lose it, and whoever loses his life will preserve it.

> This means don't think about your death; instead think about how you are living day-to-day. You will see Heaven if you are treating others the way God wants you to do, and then, you don't have to worry about your death.

> And don't think that you can live the way you want, and then in the end simply tell God you are sorry and He will save you. You don't know how you will die, if suddenly, without warning you will be gone, with no time to offer God any sorrow or repentance. Please don't let your courage to show others how fearless you are, end your life with God. Showing others that you don't have to live in God's plan, is not fearless, but grave foolishness and dangerous. Those people you are bravely trying to impress with your actions are not the ones who will come to judge you at the end of your life, or the ones who will condemn you to hell. Isn't it better to impress **The One** who will be waiting for you after death?

50

Find Friends to Follow

—Angel—original words of the plan
"Last of things for future Earth; find friends in each more so others shall follow also. Send His love upon anyone who fears/thinks God's love has no strength left; for He rebates until all ends."

—Angel—translated
Last of things for future Earth: Find friends to tell this to, so that others will follow this plan also. Send God's love through prayer to anyone who fears or thinks God's love has no strength left against what is happening on our Earth. For God will reduce the force of activity of any evil means until all ends.

Matthew 5—Jesus
Salt and Light
13 "You are the salt of the earth. But if the salt loses its saltiness, how can it be made salty again? It is no longer good for anything, except to be thrown out and trampled by men.

14 "You are the light of the world. A city on a hill cannot be hidden. 15 Neither do people light a lamp and put it under a bowl. Instead they put it on its stand, and it gives light to everyone in the house. 16 In the same way, let your light shine before men, that they may see your good deeds and praise your Father in heaven.

Psalm 40—David
9 I proclaim righteousness in the great assembly;
I do not seal my lips, as you know, O LORD.

10 I do not hide your righteousness in my heart;
I speak of your faithfulness and salvation. I do not conceal your love and your truth from the great assembly.

11 Do not withhold your mercy from me, O LORD;
may your love and your truth always protect me.

12 For troubles without number surround me;
my sins have overtaken me, and I cannot see.
They are more than the hairs of my head,
and my heart fails within me.

13 Be pleased, O LORD, to save me;
O LORD, come quickly to help me.

—God
"Go and love each other as Jesus has shown you; love also those who weep upon Earth, for they will give Our LORD good cause of saving those who weep not for justice."

Love all who weep because of them God's heart has changed to help
us.

—God
"Love all who give Our LORD hope of your return this love of He, because of them you will be saved."

Love all those who are praying for all of Earth, because of them those
who have not thought to pray will also be saved.

—God
"Love any who drive others from Me, for in them I have given all Earth My plan to courageously fight."

Love the enemy of God, because of them God has devised a new plan
for us.

—God
"Be ever more responsible with Our will of your life, for all who ask God first before making effort upon His land, will perish Earth of his evil self (Satan); because I with you along My side as you give; will change all knowledge given Earth, from forces strong against this loving plan of peace with **LORD God Almighty, We Three Us**." (We Three Us—is one of the ways God refers to the Holy Trinity, He also calls it—*God Three US, Us, Our*.)

Be aware that it is your responsibility to find out God's will for your life, because with Him at your side, you can end evil in your own life. This is what God wants all of us to do.

—God

"I know all who read this will not understand why We choose your will over this evil soul, but give Us your way for Ours to change Earth, then all will be given of you. I give this covenant with my son many times before this, he (some of mankind) I have loved; have kept My covenant of you. All else upon this planet require course against My will with them; and they I have come to save of evil dwelling among you. I give all who hear Me now, through Our daughter Carol; My blessing to live better with We who know all, and wait only of your ask for Us to bestow Our knowledge in you."

God is telling you that He has made a covenant with all of us through Jesus Christ, to end evil in our lives and give us all knowledge to live better lives. We did not fully understand the significance of what Christ was trying to show us through the way He lived, and did not understand His death to be part of a greater plan by God to free us of Satan. We chose to only take the words of Christ from the Bible and not look deeper into the way Christ lived while here. The plan God is giving us in this book is the way Christ lived while on Earth.

The son of God, Jesus, lived this covenant with God and was given all knowledge, and was protected from evil, because He did only the will of God the Father while on Earth, and taught us to do the same as He. Of course He was God, so He did have an advantage. Some that God has loved have also kept this covenant with Him. Now He has come to save the rest of us from the evil ones among us. God expected all of us to be saints, to live His way, and not find ways to make exceptions for His laws regarding how he wanted us, His children, to behave while we were using God's earthly home.

This planet is not our property, but God's. We are only allowed to use it for the few years He put us here. We were created to return love to God and to prove to Satan that loving God is all that is important in life on Earth. If we had understood all the reasons Christ came to Earth, then we would have all had more respect for God, Jesus and ourselves. Instead we have abused this planet, fought over land that is not ours to begin with, and changed God's laws in order to make ourselves more important than God. Doing all of this has jeopardized our afterlife in Heaven.

God will only allow people with pure hearts into Heaven. How pure of heart are we if we can't live with each other? How pure are our hearts if we refuse to ask God for His will of us and instead ask God to do our will? Do you think any of the souls in Heaven are not doing God's will? Oh yes, a few angels tried that and got sent here, didn't they?

God wants all of us to finally understand how to obtain our access into Heaven, and how to gain His abilities while on Earth. This will give Satan no recourse, no where to go on Earth. It will also stop the coming of David, who wants only to destroy us and watch us burn in hell. Our loving God has decided He will not let us or Earth perish the way it is currently written in the Bible, because He clearly loves us more than that.

I don't know exactly how to tell all of you that the Bible is not God's final word. He has many more words for us that are not part of this holy book, and of the past. If you elect to spend the rest of your life stuck in the past with only those teachings that you are accustomed to, you will miss out on all the wonderful knowledge that God has still to give you while you are here on Earth. This means that the Devil will have won your mind and spirit, because he will have convinced you that you can't become close to God in a personal way.

You will think that you are only allowed to have a one-way conversation with your creator, so you will go on praying for God to do your will or saying prayers that someone wrote that you only recite.

I say to all the people of this world to just give this a try. Give your soul the chance that it deserves, and your life here a chance to become whole with God. Don't let Satan convince you that all you see is all you get. God gave you so much more than meets the eye. Keep in mind that Our Creator can do anything, at any time of history, and because His love for us is unlimited, He doesn't need to limit Himself to only what is written in the Bible. God can give us all we need—at all times—with no consideration to the past, whatsoever.

When The LORD comes to Earth to ask for your will of Him, you will marvel at what He will show you that did not meet the eye. There will be tears of joy and pain that day; there will also be fear like you have never experienced. Even the bravest of them all will quiver in fear. I can tell you that since God gave me this message in April of 2006, I have experienced both tears of joy and pain, as God talks to me and explains His way. I cry at the amount of love God has for us, and the amount of pain He has endured at our neglect of Him.

For no other reason than your love for God, I implore you to give this plan your greatest effort of your life. Then receive from God all the blessings He has waiting for you.

—God—continued
"I leave you these words as a way of life. Any who live Our way, die of Us in them and will live of Us all eternity. For only in Us can Heaven bring forth eternal pleasures untold of any who know them. Only in We who give life can life abounding be given. All mankind is now Our way, so evil has no place else upon Our planet."

—God
"I will this give you, when you say of Me; Thy will is done."

It is God's will that we show our love for Him through this plan. He wishes us to rid Earth of evil by giving Him our freewill and doing only His will for us.

If this happens as God planned it to, all Earth will cast Satan away from us, leaving his soul no where on Earth left to go. God will then bless Earth abundantly, until He decides to take us to live in Heaven with Him. When all Earth has cast Satan from our lives, we can all say to God, "Thy will is done."

—God
"Our LORD gives us all knowledge; we with God need only give our will of He to access all He offers us."

Photo taken by The Bellman, in 2004 Public Domain

Of course, I asked God before I put these words on this photo;
He laughed and said He liked it.

The Ten Commandments

Deuteronomy 6—Moses

4 Hear, O Israel: The LORD our God, the LORD is one. 5 Love the LORD your God with all your heart and with all your soul and with all your strength. 6 These commandments that I give you today are to be upon your hearts. 7 Impress them on your children. Talk about them when you sit at home and when you walk along the road, when you lie down and when you get up. 8 Tie them as symbols on your hands and bind them on your foreheads. 9 Write them on the doorframes of your houses and on your gates.

Gustave Doré 1833-1883 Public Domain

Matthew 22—Jesus

36 "Teacher, which is the greatest commandment in the Law?" 37 Jesus replied: "'Love the Lord your God with all your heart and with all your soul and with all your mind. 38 This is the first and greatest commandment. 39 And the second is like it: 'Love your neighbor as yourself.' 40 All the Law and the Prophets hang on these two commandments."

—God

"In view of what I am teaching My loved souls of Earth, in this book, to come only unto God for all you require in your life; I am clearing up the confusion of how to honor Me, through keeping My Commandments, that were always your way of giving Me the honor and love I needed from you.

"I created man to form a circle of love between My children of Earth, who I love greatly, even more than mankind could understand of love; and their God, who offers them all they need to survive on this Earth. "In these commands, I gave them ways to give of each other so that none will be without Me around their life.

I did not give these to frighten My children into obedience; but to show them that through love of Me, they can live peacefully on My Earth.

"My children never understood how following these laws would make their lives fuller and their thoughts richer, so that they could be ready to come of Heaven, where all is pure and holy. Instead, they take My laws as hardships for them to follow. They feel this way because following these laws requires them to give up the deeds encouraged by Satan, that make them feel good about their presence on Earth, through false judgments of themselves and their neighbor.

"My children have not, in all these years of Earth, known that God is not their enemy of what is good about Earth. Your Earth is My joy and your lives My most important thoughts. So when you judge the evil pleasures of Earth, as the most pleasing feelings of your life, then I know you do not understand the pleasures of God that follow this life. You have been deceived by Satan to believe what you feel on Earth is all that consists in the realm of feeling, which is not so.

"Earth feelings are limited to the body you are given, the knowledge you are given, and the perceptions allowed you by Me. So Satan can convince you that the pleasures you get while on Earth are all there is. In reality, Satan is giving you only a minute amount of pleasure and all other pleasures of mind and soul, and even body are given by God. You can not know how deceived you have been, if you continue to do as Satan tempts you to do; only by coming into your Father's knowledge, can you know what you are missing.

"For this reason of your teaching within this book, I am going to give you My Commandments again, with all corrections made of what has been changed of them, to satisfy those who choose their will over My will. I say to all of you who have chosen to misguide others with these changes, that you do mankind a huge injustice of eliminating God from their lives, by offering them alternatives to My laws.

"These truths were made to give happiness to My children, and not to give them sorrow about their lives on Earth. Satan has come to give them sorrow about not keeping My laws. Satan knows that to tempt My children away from My way; is to confuse and discourage them, to a point that they feel being bad and evil makes you feel good, and being holy makes you feel lonely and empty on Earth.

"All evil is from Satan, and all good is from God. All love is from God. So when you do evil, and do not find love in your life, how then can you call your life fun and enjoyable? What is so enjoyable about a loveless life? How do you intend to fulfill My will of you, if you bring evil to your life without regard of Me?

197

"This is how I have asked My beloved Moses to give My commands of you. I now ask My daughter of Earth beings, to fulfill her promise of Me, to give all I have said to her. I tell you she is of many doubts, for these will give her members of life, sadness and worry to read My meanings. Many things require change and people of Earth will need to adjust their lives to give Me honor as I have asked. Our child is of sadness herself at a loss of those things that were thought good of God. But now I tell her why I do not find these pure and holy in my site.

"I say one thing more of these changes; today I ask Earth to give back to God what is proper for life with Me in Heaven. You have lived too long of Satan's way, and souls are in My Purgatory of souls, to wash away these evil actions, before I grant them Us in Heaven. I forgive those who come of Me to ask pardon for these actions taken against Me, but those who never believe them wrong because authorities of Earth have given them abilities to justify what is incorrect of Heavenly God; will suffer Purgatory, until given rights by Us to enter Our home.

I will give Our daughter, Our thoughts for answering questions of Our will for your lives with Us. Give her your regard on matters of Us, for no other will be given these answers for your Earth. This is My word of this matter."

Deuteronomy 5:6-21

ONE: 6"I am the LORD your God, 7"You shall have no other gods before me."

—God 9-7-2006
"This is say to My people who I have created. Many years ago when Earth was created, I gave orders of Adam and Eve to live according to My laws for them. They were My beloved human beings, who God your Master Almighty above, created to bring Him love above all else given them.

"But as Satan came upon them, fighting Me with evil, these human beings changed of Me. They took word of Satan over Mine. They obey his command of them, before Me. This is what is meant by no other gods before Me. Satan takes all away from God. He is not your creator, nor your master of your life force. This of Me is precious gift, bestowed on your life. Anything that changed you from My love is considered of Me as a false god, and I forbid mankind to take these interest before Me.

"I say be careful who you listen to, be it family or friend, preacher or Satan. If any say against My laws, they are false god for you. Do not listen of them; do not give them your time or your knowledge. Do not work for them, or work with them. Do not buy their wares or go to their businesses. Do not give them what only belongs to God."

8 **"You shall not make for yourself an idol in the form of anything in heaven above or on the earth beneath or in the waters below.** 9 You shall not bow down to them or worship them; for I, the LORD your God, am a jealous God, punishing the children for the sin of the fathers to the third and fourth generation of those who hate me, 10 but showing love to a thousand generations of those who love me and keep my commandments.

—God 9-7-2006

"I say to all mankind, this day in your year. When you take clay, wood, rock or paper into your hand and draw or carve of it any form other than the Son of God or Mother be this Son, Mary; then you have struck the will of God from your heart.

"I give My command of this day to destroy all images made of saints above and people who have been living upon Earth, that grace your alters and churches to bear images to ask intercession of Me; for all other images made are forbidden, as I have stated long ago.

"You disgrace yourself in front of God, when you pray of these images made of beings past. None but Our LORD's image should show in churches, where man brings love to God. This I say, as a way to let you know that you should not be offering prayer for favors of life, to any of those who have gone before you. I am your LORD God of all mankind and I am the only one who answers your prayers.

"Be kind of each other while you are destroying these images, so that none with you are encouraging others of wrongdoing, for God judges all men the same when this happens."

—Carol—Question to God

"Can these images be sent to museums so as not to lose the beauty of the art form?"

—God's answer

"I will allow these to be saved, only if they be removed from all churches immediately and given of museums without payment for viewing them. These of Earth should remain earthly, without grievance of Me, by giving them reason for greed of some. No sale should be made of them to each museum and no payment asked of any who choose to view them. This is how I only allow them saved."

—Carol—Question to God
"God, can these images be put into a church vestibule or outdoor park?"

—God's answer
"Child, give these images your consideration of Me. I tell you that only in a place away from my house, with no effort given of prayer to them, can they exist at all."

. . . .

TWO: 11 "You shall not misuse the name of the LORD your God, for the LORD will not hold anyone guiltless who misuses his name.

—God 9-7-2006
"This is important to remember all times. I have seen many of Earth use the name of God in curse of everything made of Me. I am all things of Earth. You need remember that when you curse My man of Earth, you curse Me; when you curse My land or My wares, you curse Me also. There is none allowed by Me, to use the name of God in this manner.

"Also I tell you that My name is holy and sacred and should you use it for bringing harm against another, or blasphemy; I will end your life of Me. No man is to use the LORD your God, in any improper manner, or life will be ended with Us in Heaven. No more is said of this now."

. . . .

THREE: 12 "Observe the Sabbath day by keeping it holy, as the LORD your God has commanded you. 13 Six days you shall labor and do all your work, 14 but the seventh day is a Sabbath to the LORD your God. On it you shall not do any work, neither you, nor your son or daughter, nor your manservant or maidservant, nor your ox, your donkey or any of your animals, nor the alien within your gates, so that your manservant and maidservant may rest, as you do.

—God 9-7-2006
"All of Earth should know My way is to give you a day to rest from all your problems given you from hard work. So I say of you take this day I give you,

for your body and soul to come of Me for replenishment of both. For even God needed rest to view all that was done of that week.

"Review what you have accomplished during your week and how you have served the LORD in what you have done. If you see no glory for God in your work, then no accomplishment was done at all. For all Earth is My belonging and all man is My child. So all done to man and for man is done for Me alone. Give all to God and God will give you everything you need each day.

"Many of you have changed this practice of keeping this day holy. I allow good acts of mercy be done, and forbid stores to open for sale of anything not required when body is at rest. Remember that if you are home reviewing your week, then you don't require many things given you.

"If you open your businesses and require employees to disregard My command of them, I will count this as your sin against Me. They will not be judged of what you have forced them of doing. This does not give you rights to change My command of them. They are your workers and I am your God. If you force people to work when they know of My command, you will give Me reason to take action against your business. For My laws come first, always.

"Give of My command all your knowledge and desire toward your work schedule and for your honor of Me, your business will prosper greatly. Give no regard of Me and I give no regard of your hopes for profit."

. . . .

FOUR: 16 "Honor your father and your mother, as the LORD your God has commanded you, so that you may live long and that it may go well with you in the land the LORD your God is giving you.

—God 9-7-2006
"How can this be different than My original meaning? Give your parents your respect, because I have given these people a holy practice of giving children homes, with good knowledge, and proper food and dress. I do not give all means to support your upbringing, but give blessings of those who suffer to complete this work given them, through Me.

"All children given are at My will. All parents granted My will of these children are in direct response of My will. You as My children are responsible for those I leave in your care. So parent; take care of your children as I would care for them, and child of parent; take care of your father and mother until I choose of their end.

"This is My command to you. Care of both child and parent, does not mean send them off as if not your concern. I, your God say they are your concern that needs love, trust and permanent means of honor by you. Never give up this honor given you to some caretaker and think I approve this act. You are the ones love should be given by and to. For this way Heaven will be waiting for you; who show Me, that when you come unto Me, your heavenly Father, you have given and received love and know how to give this also of Me."

Matthew 15—Jesus

4 For God said, 'Honor your father and mother' and 'Anyone who curses his father or mother must be put to death.' 5 But you say that if a man says to his father or mother, 'Whatever help you might otherwise have received from me is a gift devoted to God,' 6 he is not to 'honor his father' with it. Thus you nullify the word of God for the sake of your tradition.

. . . .

FIVE: 17 "You shall not murder. (Kill)

—God 9-7-2006

"I am very disappointed with My children on this respect. I gave this law for one purpose only. To give all Earth My command to love and respect what I have given as life. Do you take My gift so disrespectfully of Me, that you increase knowledge of Me to include justice as your own to give?

"Do you think you are able to judge one of My children so fully; as to be able to say this child should not exist of us, who are perfect in the eyes of God? What has one of your own done, that God cannot forgive? I say of all who listen to My word today.

I do not give this judgment easily as you do. None of Me, will perish until all of Heaven is done in their respect to save them of hell.

"I tell you this strongly; you cannot give an order to kill one of My children without coming to Me to offer yourself in his place. If you take a life of Mine, from this Earth, you give your life to Me as well, to do with as I see fit of you.

"This is said of any circumstance upon this Earth. I do not give special favor to those in war, or offended by another. I give no offer to those policing streets or court-appointed. I say to all My children, no matter where or when you offend Me, by this crime against Me, I will punish you in the same manor as you give.

"So this is your answer now: Give every respect of any who offend you; for I will judge them, on what they did to one who belongs to Me. But should you judge over Me, their mistakes; I will judge you worse offender of both.

"I see you have chosen to forget this commandment in many instances. I will give My order of this against all you choose that I forbid of you, once again.

"No abortion is made of any child; I give when conceived and will not offer any this end. I say that birth control is God's domain. I give, when I have need of love, for all life is a circle of love between a child and Me.

"Who among you has the right to say of God, 'You do not need love brought through Me'? Birth control of mankind is simply restrain of your practice of sex. No means of taking life away from God is appropriate. I have given sexual means solely to populate my Earth. Other means done of this is inappropriate form, in the eyes of God.

"No court shall give the order to kill alone. All who witness in court must stand in full knowledge at any death of them. I say if one deserves to die, any who accuse this one, must offer his hand to take this life, or none will take his life. Give of prison instead.

"No one angry of another will strike down his enemy. When one is against you, I am with you and see everything taking place. I then will judge this one who offends you and call upon him My answer to his life. If you come before Me to judge he who offends you, you offend God in the practice and I will come to judge you also. Stay clear of My judgment of your actions.

"No one deserves war at his or her hand. Many die of those who strike against their enemy; and I see innocent lives taken when none should be gone of Earth. My child is in My hands and of My will of him, so when you send of war unwarranted by Me, you take his life out of My hands and you take My authority over his life, away from Me.

"I do not look upon this action without holding you responsible to Heaven. See fit that you take every other means before ordering your people to war. I say also that should you think you need war, then you should be asking your God, who should be allowed of this? All life is precious to Me, and all souls given My love over all else. You cannot say if war is needed. I am the only one who can say all else is done and only war will end this correctly.

"No form child of body parts. This is when one part of one soul is given to save another. I will say who is saved and who is not. You are not to act Godly and make parts for each other of human tissue. None I tell you. This is not negotiable with Heaven. This is a form Satan uses to make God less important in your life. You are not of My will in this case."

—Carol—question to God
"Do you also mean transplants of body parts, like hearts, lungs, blood, etc? Or do you just mean the forming of new life or the cell work being done now?"

—God—answer
"Why do you think I would allow My children to share parts I have given them? I give as Myself to each child on Earth. They think it is My answer to share out of love for one another to save a life.

"But God does not want this sharing done for this reason. When spirits of evil means come into one close to death, they make that soul go of them for life. You see a way to save yourself and offer your good will of God up, to those who offer parts of life, as means of saving you. But God is able alone to save your life without pieces offered you.

"See what sharing of parts has done of some that ask of them. They thank each other for life, but not He who have come to their aid. They thank their doctors for life, and do not give God authority over them as should be. I tell you that your God has all you need for life. Man does not have to pretend to place their efforts for self-pride and self-satisfaction above what God gives. These of man are wrong choices, given by Satan, to show God how His way is not needed over man."

—Carol—question
"Even, blood transfusions?"

—God—answer
"I say you open yourself up for many illness problems, due to these forms of blood transfer. I give life, when life is accepted with Me. I take life, no matter

which form of transfusion occurs within a soul of Mine, if that is My will, and I see a better way for this soul to serve Me. Tell Me Carol, what do you want life to be for those who become ill?"

—Carol—answer
"I am not sure, God. Just life that will give them time on Earth, I guess."

—God—response
"Then you see dear child, life without will of God is only vegetation of source formed of man. You can not predict My answer for them, so why save what you can not know. If My child requires Me for life, then life is worth living. If his life requires another, then his life is already dead of Me. So too, his body should die.

These things your generation has considered a blessing of Me in wrong thinking. I am changing this of now.

"Also I say of death by terrorizing. I forbid this in every way. My children will not be given this treatment, from they who listen of evil means to persuade life their way. This of them is very bad thinking and will stop now. I give no order for holy wars done of Me. I have not ever given order of this means. This is means with Satan, at thought to give God as war.

"Your God is not evil this way. I am love only. I tell you all this with great sorrow, that I see mankind feel Me as give death in horrid form. I do not give this end of any, but Satan gives and tells all; this is what I want. How does mankind believe this of Me; over what I say of My love of them?".

> I can't read this last paragraph without crying. While God was telling me of His sorrow, I could feel the shift in His energy to great pain and sorrow. I wish those who are so involved in this form of killing, could feel this sorrow in them.

> Our loving Father would never ask for a holy war. God wins people over through love. If you kill someone before God has done everything He wills, to save them from hell, you have done so against the will of God, and given God reason to judge you, for that death.

> I pray that through these words from God that anyone involved in forcing another to bend to their will; can see that war is not God's answer.

Prayer for a Spouse

I ask You LORD to send my spouse,
In he I am complete,
But give him heart that beats for me,
And gives good will for Thee.

Send just the person made in Thee
With charm that warms my soul to Thee;
Of lips that speak nice words in he,
Of arms well fixed for chastity,
And legs straight forth in work they be,
And mind of sole encharity.

So when we mate our souls entwine,
Our hearts enlight our system chime,
In we is God aloof of time;

For when we meet is just retreat,
Of when our life be more complete
Sweet Jesus say You bless of we.

. . . .

SIX: 18 "You shall not commit adultery.

—God 9-7-2006
"How is it, that mankind thinks God would allow so many to commit this offense against Me? I say to you now, the meaning of adultery is this; give yourself of only your own wife or husband. If you are joined of Me through marriage in My name, then stay with that one who is your half. If your half should give of self to another then you can leave this one, for this reason only.

"But should your half be of faithful to your vow of them, you cannot give of yourself to another, no matter if you live of your wife or not. (This is regarding separation)You are not divorce of a faithful spouse, in the eyes of the LORD.

"I say of My churches, who offer means of ending an unfaithful marriage. If this couple has children they are not to be said annulled of this marriage within the church. How of Us is this possible to say that they are not joined of them, when a child is made of their marriage? Say only that they can come of church when need of Me in their life. I give no child of Mine reason not to come of Me. I know that many will fall under the evil of Satan, so I tell you that in My eyes they remain married.

"The one who is not at fault of this sin is of My will to come to Me in church and receive all goodness of God. The one who is in sin with this and gives reason to separate from his spouse, is not allowed of My church, until he has come for forgiveness and repents his wrongdoing with no effort of any other person. (This means you must go to God in remorse of your sins, not because someone told you that you have to ask forgiveness. Also it means that you cannot have a girlfriend or boyfriend that you intend to sleep with or marry.) They are not allowed to remarry, for I do not give my blessing on two marriages at the same time."

For couples with children.

God does not consider them divorced or annulled. Even if one is unfaithful, God considers your marriage intact. However, the unfaithful person cannot go to church until that person asks forgiveness and repents their sin against God.

You cannot get divorced, and no marriage can be annulled if children were born of these two people. You were given a child by God to raise and that child given you to take care of in your old age. (Honor thy father and thy mother and thy child). You can live separately if one is unfaithful, but you cannot marry another because God will not give His blessings for two marriages at the same time. And remember God considers you still married.

The bottom line here is this: be very careful before you marry, because there is no way out that is approved by God. If you want to live separate, you can, but, you cannot have sex or marriage with another.

God is willing to forgive any sins; if we ask for forgiveness.

—Carol—question
"What if both are unfaithful?"

—God—answer
"My daughter is giving Me your doubt of My command so that she may clear this matter of Me. So I say unto you who wish to get around My law of this, by committing even more offense against Me, so that you can divorce; I forbid you to divorce under any circumstance if you have children given to you out of love from God."

—God—continued

"If two marry and have no children and one is unfaithful, they can be divorced but only the one who remained faithful is without sin, and can become as single again without asking forgiveness before coming of Me. The other must come for forgiveness of sins against Me and then I will give My way of him or her again. *This is how I want My people to live of My new plan of their lives. You must come of Me alone, to know if God wills you ending your marriage.*"

If you have no children, God will allow divorce, and the person who has not sinned against God can remarry without remorse. But the person who was unfaithful must go to God for forgiveness and repent before God will allow him or her to come into church again.

However, as this plan explains, before you get divorced from anyone, you must come to God to find out if it is the will of God that you divorce. God will know if your problems can be worked out and your love rekindled. Don't just hurriedly separate; what brought you together in the first place may be more important than forgiving the unfaithful person. Remember if God can forgive this person, then so can you.

If you divorce you are considered single and you follow the guidelines God has for single people again.

—God—Continued

"As for single people, I say one thing: You are to remain sexless; of this I give no recourse or change."

"No man shall take a woman who is virgin; or stain of her womb shall curse your end." (We are talking single people here, not a married couple)

"No child shall be united with an adult for sexual reasons." (Single or married and as God puts it; woe to you if you take the innocence of a child of God.)

"No women, of middle age, waste her days bringing men pleasures alone, if never before brought of men for this reason. For I see all that happens on my Earth. If no man asks your hand in marriage, then all remain only single woman. I forbid these women to mate with men who refuse marriage, in place of sexual desires to many women. This of God is intolerable behavior for both man and woman. I see this behavior as normal pleasure over the entire world and I say this to all who currently disobey my laws of this; repent of this and ask forgiveness for Heaven belongs only to pure souls, who offer God their will power over themselves, and just these who give this way. I do not offer men or women my home for giving Me sites of them in sin."

We have been duped by Satan into thinking this world is made for our pleasures of the body. In this world, today nearly everything you see and hear ignites your senses and directs you toward sex. I know this is one of our most enjoyable gifts from God, but Satan has made it his favorite act of hatred against Our LORD, and is using us to carry out his evil deeds. Each time we fall into his traps, we hurt God, Our Creator, and please Satan, because he knows we just keep justifying this act of sex for ourselves.

This commandment covers our clothing used to entice others, the TV and commercials we watch, the movies we see, the books we read, and the internet sites.

It also covers same-sex acts, masturbation, and incest; as well as rape, especially of virgins; taking the purity of a child, and God knows there are more women in the world then men, and is not allowing you to take advantage of that fact. For women who never marry, you are never allowed sex no matter what Satan tells you about your time running out to have children.

I know this is a harsh statement to be said in this day and age. However, you must remember that God does not see Earth as different than when He created it. He destroyed the Earth in Noah's day, and then Sodom and Gomorrah for the same thing He sees today. So you can not use the excuse that this is the 21st century, to God. He will simply come back with, "So you have had 20 centuries to learn how I feel about what you are doing."

—Carol—question asked in Morning Prayer with God
"Same-sex and other sexual practices?"

—God's answer
"I have given our Earth, for many years, laws to govern sexual behavior. This I have put down in word of Me through His most glorified name. Our God is against same sexual drive for these ways.

"First, He sees both partners being cowardly about women and men of their opposite. This is why choose our own.

"Second, no child can come of this.

Third, no law of God forgives of these souls, for God know of what make them hungry of this. (Satan) They offer no good gift toward glorify God, when this action has taken place.

"God give sexual intercourse for purpose to populate Earth only. All else He wish not done; for none other reason give grace for you. Go tell this of His way."

Deuteronomy 22—**Law's given to Moses**
5 A woman must not wear men's clothing, nor a man wear women's clothing, for the LORD your God detests anyone who does this.

Leviticus 18—**Law's given to Moses**
6 "No one is to approach any close relative to have sexual relations. I am the LORD."
7 "Do not dishonor your father by having sexual relations with your mother. She is your mother; do not have relations with her."
8 "Do not have sexual relations with your father's wife; that would dishonor your father."
9 "Do not have sexual relations with your sister, either your father's daughter or your mother's daughter, whether she was born in the same home or elsewhere."
10 "Do not have sexual relations with your son's daughter or your daughter's daughter; that would dishonor you.'
11 "Do not have sexual relations with the daughter of your father's wife, born to your father she is your sister."
12 "Do not have sexual relations with your father's sister; she is your father's close. relative."
13 "Do not have sexual relations with your mother's sister, because she is your mother's close relative."
14 "Do not dishonor your father's brother by approaching his wife to have sexual relations; she is your aunt."
15 "Do not have sexual relations with your daughter-in-law. She is your son's wife; do not have relations with her."
16 "Do not have sexual relations with your brother's wife; that would dishonor your brother."
17 "Do not have sexual relations with both a woman and her daughter. Do not have sexual relations with either her son's daughter or her daughter's daughter; they are her close relatives. That is wickedness."
18 "Do not take your wife's sister as a rival wife and have sexual relations with her while your wife is living."
19 "Do not approach a woman to have sexual relations during the uncleanness of her monthly period."

20 "Do not have sexual relations with your neighbor's wife and defile yourself with her."

21 "Do not give any of your children to be sacrificed to Molech, for you must not profane the name of your God. I am the LORD."

22 "Do not lie with a man as one lies with a woman; that is detestable."

23 "Do not have sexual relations with an animal and defile yourself with it. A woman must not present herself to an animal to have sexual relations with it; that is a perversion."

• •

mustard seed 9/13/2006
"You asked me yesterday if masturbating was a sin. I asked God today."

mustard seed "Father, is masturbating a sin?"

—God—answer
"I will say the truth regarding this means of pleasure self. When I say no one is to regard life fully aware of his end, then I mean you will not know when God will take you from Earth to live of Us, with all goodness given you. So I say this much of those who try My wits end with self-adjustments toward pleasing of self. If I come of you in this act; I leave to find another in your place. Then I take (that person) of my home. You, I let wait of My honor. So when I say, no one should give pleasure in this fashion, I say so, only for this means give no thought over Earth purpose of God. I say this is no sin of yourself; however, it is no great pleasure to God.

"Go do what pleases God first in all cases; then pleasure self, of love for self, if none with Earth are your pleasure. This of us will be tolerated, but never approved. I say one thing more regarding this means; be careful of whom you adjust your mind about, for all thoughts of none with your wife, will bring sin against you. Better you think of no one of source near you, than one who comes close of your home. These be adjusted in mind mental of body, with no problems given of your life"

> Do you understand? Do not masturbate thinking of anyone who is within your reach, unless it is your own spouse. And if you think you could die soon, don't do it or God will pass you by, rather than come for you at that time. Hahahaha

mustard seed Don't you just love Our God?

• •

—God

"One thing you must remember throughout your life. When I give you challenges of Me, as I am right now, I give you blessings to fulfill these images done by you, on My behalf. I do not leave My children without means to fulfill My will for them.

"Your lives are changed for evil, by Satan's touch of your will over Mine. Satan then leaves you in desire of more pleasures of the flesh and mind. But as you turn your hearts of Me and forget this evil soul's thoughts; you will have more love to sustain you until you become as My will of your life should be.

"Do not fear this change, as I know most of you who feel this is all you have to enjoy in this life, will come to think. This also is brought to you by his evil self, to make you fear Us. I do not harm My children; I am here with you to rescue your souls from hell, not to give you pain and suffering while on Earth. My will of you comes through love for all mankind. Satan comes only of hatred to all and ends his plan of you, only when he has taken your soul to hell."

Adultery Poem

Two people in love are said,
To give of love empowered;
But three people of love are both in need
Of one who wants an end for thee.

So never choose for who to see
Of more than one alone with thee,
For God will give you tyranny,
For breathing life away from He;

Give only just respect of He,
For in this life is only me,
Your friend or spouse eternally.
Of course you will abandon three.

. . . .

SEVEN: 19 "You shall not steal.

—God 9-8-2006

"Of all of Our Commandments, this is most misused. I gave you this law to keep you from hurting each other in business and daily practice of giving each other what is rightfully yours to give.

"So this is now Our word regarding this law; do not cheat each other of any product produced in your name. This includes food products brought to Our children when you have not grown them. I give My children Earth products natural of man and some of you think that because you bottle these and produce title to them, that you own them.

"You can not own My Earth, nor My water, grapes of wild grown, My fields of flowers for smell and touch, My orchards grown in natural settings, My earth worms or graves dug.

"I say to you, that all Earth for burial purpose is exposed to evil beings that prey on poor of this Earth, by overcharging them for funerals, flashy and over-barring in state made of them. My children are dead of body and require little done of their body more. I give them grounds for burial, so charge only what is rightfully yours in these instances.

"Again I say to you, that giving others rights over dead beings is incorrect of Us. Undertakers of your years are giving many small amounts in home in order to take incomes for burial purpose. I regard this shameful behavior of their part. For I say to all of you, that ground made for burial is required to all human beings, and because all need of this, price should remain small. My thought of this should remain large in your minds."

> It doesn't look like God is very happy about pre-planned funerals or insurance that takes money needed for living and gives it to over-barring funerals. Burial should be less flashy in God's mind.

"I see children (God's children) take what belongs of others in their households and businesses and bring to place they hide until say of others; this is mine. I control for you now, who is doing this means of error on My laws.

"Children small of age, see adults giving them items taken from others and expressing good reward. How then can child learn that this be incorrect behavior if you say I reward you in this way?"

> If you are taking little things from work and giving them to your children when you get home, you are teaching them that stealing is a good thing.

"I see adults take of articles placed in hotel rooms for guest use and carry these off as if not done in remiss of it.

"I see business person charge more of items than worth in market and give no remiss.

"I see state officers claim good work done of they; and take incomes granted them by citizens who trust in them, but see no wrong in their actions.

"I have given My churches courage to ask parishioners of income granted of those who do good work of LORD God, but see them waste of this income to replace many items, not broken or worn, to satisfy congregations' rich course.

"I see many chapels build in much pomp of they who dwell there. I give no order for fancy place for pray. I say pray of your humility, and leave this array of glory, for My home in Heaven. Earth needs not glory of buildings, only glory with God.

"I see many give each other discount of items, they should not have priced so high of first place. So as to make others think they are good of will towards them. In Our site, they steal from impoverished beings to satisfy wealthy ones.

"I see government agencies take taxes unwarranted to increase revenue to wealthy business owners asking for government help; while the poor of the Earth go without necessities of life to bring wealthy ones increased amounts.

"I say to you, that your income should be in direct reflection of your work in every state of business. When one works toward his end, then income should justify his effort, but with some of this Earth, income is far beyond their worth to any of God's people. **So beyond My view of yourself, you follow Satan's justification of life.**

"On this Earth today, many of My children suffer of illness, unable to pay the price for services and medications. Drug companies offer drugs unsuitable of Us; that affect My people in offensive ways and change their lives of Us; because given a drug that allows evil dwellers to increase pressure over them, who are too weak to fight this. I say; spend your time in thought about what you offer to many for I will offer their lives for yours should they expire of your means.

"Be of good form when giving pills to little ones of Earth also, for their bodies can't fight off what is good for adults with little hope. I give them more healing power and they can withstand illness not given older persons.

"I say, you of the industries, that My children rely on daily for successful life on Earth, are My worst offenders. You see need and greed takes your hearts to pressure all into giving more to your will than to My will for them. You who offer food and clothing are giving many bad choices and regardless of this, you charge very high prices, so that only those who find work more can afford your items. I say to you, when I give someone ability to provide of all children on Earth, and you pick who you will offer your work product to, then you give Me reason to forbid you make these products.

"I give knowledge and ability to be shared with even the least of My children who has no ability at all.

"When you take food away of some, you cause illness to them, and should they die of this, your life is their reward of Me.

"When you take clothing off the backs of those who are poor, I allow you cold wind to live in.

"When you give many bad drugs, I allow you illness to give you reason to replace good for bad.

"When you say earn less; I give less in your knowledge so that you are aware of less.

"None can steal from God and get away with it. When you take from My children in any way, you take from Me also. I then adjust that part of your life to give you a reason to change all evil you are doing.

"Think of how you are getting what you have in life. If what you have comes from evil means then you are stealing life away from someone. You are taking someone else's good money for your evil means. I say to you, I do not see this matter end well for you. Stealing consists of any means gotten through evil means. Before you justify your means ask yourself, are these just with God. If you can not say they are, then know God will justify them for you with other means brought into your life.

"I give those with My will for them, all they need to survive this life and live according to My will of them. If your life is full of wealth horded in banks and businesses and property so that none of Earth can touch it, then My will of you has failed you. Your wealth is not the will of God, it is help given of Satan, to bring your heart away from God, who loves all His children and wants all to be in Heaven at the end of their life. I have told My Earth that wealth is God's enemy, because those who horde money on Earth spend only what is needed to satisfy their own happiness. But those who spend all they have to bring happiness to others are hording rewards of Us in Heaven."

> What can I add to this? God has broadened stealing to every means of making money in life. If your income doesn't justify the means you use to get that income, God says you are stealing. If your income is way out of proportion to the amount of work you need to do to make that income, then you are stealing because your income is coming out of the mouths and hands of someone that needs that money. Someone is being used in a wrong way to get that money to you. God will not justify your large income at the expense of those who are really paying for it.

> So what are we talking about here? Gas, entertainment, food, clothing, medical, insurance, school supplies, building supplies, etc.; everything needed in life. If your income is out of proportion to the work you do, then someone is suffering to give that income to you. God sees everything, and knows if you are offering your employees large amounts of money by taking advantage of someone else.

. . . .

EIGHT: 20 "You shall not give false testimony against your neighbor.

—God 9-8-2006
"I say this to everyone; you can not say things about each other, to other people even if you think you are doing right by the person you talk to. If what you say is found wrong by Me, I will judge you of this.

"You do not know every circumstance of a situation you are talking about with someone else. You bring others to judgment with your neighbor when you gossip about them even as humor.

"So I tell you that this law is not of testify in court alone, it is testify of your neighbor under any circumstance done. Be it in voice, or in writing of his name. I will also judge your actions strong if you give others cause to look for wrongdoings of another, without full knowledge of a situation. It is very hard for mankind to know all about another's thoughts and actions.

"This is why **when you live in My way,** with God united with your every thought, you will not give false witness of others, because your only concern will be that of your life with God. **You will not see others outside of your love for God."**

Stay away from the water cooler, God is watching; at work, in your neighborhood, with relatives, with friends, etc.

Okay, for all of those in the news business, pay attention. God is talking to you. As far as God is concerned, you do not have a right to write or talk about your neighbor without knowing every circumstance and detail truthfully. God is also telling you that for mankind to know every detail would be pretty much impossible.

You can talk all you want about the right to know and the laws of your countries, but God is judging you in regard to what you are saying and who you are taking pictures of, that will cause others to bring judgment about the person you are talking about. It is evil to present even facts that cause someone else to judge another, because, God is the only one who knows enough about the circumstances to be able to judge anyone. When you start to see evil spirits around people, then you can judge them, until then, you better let God handle it.

In addition, be careful when presenting reality shows and talk shows and comedy shows, and political campaigns. Be extremely careful about what you present in 30 seconds, 60 seconds, a half hour or hour about someone else's life. No amount of money is going to be worth a bad judgment by God. You might be better off sticking to talking about your own life and leaving other people's lives out of your comment.

Remember: All of us need to be very careful about what we are saying about others and what we are presenting to the world about someone else. This might be a good time to start planning a new TV line up, or a new type of newspaper that looks for the good in someone.

. . . .

NINE: ₂₁ **"You shall not covet your neighbor's wife.**

TEN: You shall not set your desire on your neighbor's house or land, his manservant or maidservant, his ox or donkey, or anything that belongs to your neighbor."

—God 9-8-2006

"This of Us in Heaven, refers to loving self enough to ask Our LORD your course for life on Earth. When you offer your will for Ours, you need not look of others for your joys of Earth. You need only see what God wills of your work and life. So, no need of looking toward others for excuses of change for your life.

"This sin refers to being unhappy of your place in life. This be jealousy of those around you, and is referred to by Us as **'Prostitution Of Earth'**. When man knows his place then all is good in his heart and mind, when you lose your will of Us, because you forget who you are in relationship to Our will with you, then you allow others yourself to use, until you find your proper place again."

This commandment shows you when your life is incomplete. If you desire what someone else has, then you have no understanding of what God wants you to be doing in this life. You are wandering mindlessly through life until you offer God your freewill and allow Him to tell you what your purpose is on a daily basis. God will simply wait for you to do this. Satan being as opportunistic as he is, takes advantage of this situation and will send you all sorts of little signals, to entice you to grab what is around you, telling you that these things will give you pleasure. God calls this "Prostitution of Earth," meaning you prostitute yourself out to anyone or anything that offers you money or pleasure, because you can't see your true worth, without seeing yourself through God's vision of you. No one else can show you what you are capable of doing, or capable of being except God, who planned your life and gave you all the abilities to complete His plan for you, from conception through eternity.

But as one, who is united with God, I can tell you with absolute confidence, that nothing gives you pleasure like knowing you are fulfilling God's will, and God is telling you good job. Nothing on Earth compares to the feeling you will get when you know your creator, your heavenly Father has graced you with His blessings. This I assure you is better than sex and/or money.

I only wish I could somehow give all of you knowledge of what God's energy feels like around you. If I could, not one of you would doubt one second that doing God's will is preferable to anything you have experienced. This is one reason I told God immediately that I would bring His words to the world. I just want all of us to be as blessed by God as I am, and feel what I feel in God's presence; this would be a wonderful experience for us to share. I'd like to add: If Heaven is better than this feeling, (I am told that Heaven is a glorious place.) then I implore all of you to do everything you can to get there.

There are over 200 passages, in the Bible, that speak about the importance of keeping God's Commandments.

Leviticus 19—Various Laws given to Moses

1 The LORD said to Moses, "Speak to the entire assembly of Israel and say to them: 'Be holy because I, the LORD your God, am holy.'"

3 "Each of you must respect his mother and father, and you must observe My Sabbaths. I am the LORD your God."

4 "Do not turn to idols or make gods of cast metal for you. I am the LORD your God."

9 "When you reap the harvest of your land, do not reap to the very edges of your field or gather the gleanings of your harvest."

10 "Do not go over your vineyard a second time or pick up the grapes that have fallen. Leave them for the poor and the alien. I am the LORD your God."

11 "Do not steal."

"Do not lie."

"Do not deceive one another."

12 "Do not swear falsely by my name and so profane the name of your God. I am the LORD."

13 "Do not defraud your neighbor or rob him."

"Do not hold back the wages of a hired man overnight."

14 "Do not curse the deaf or put a stumbling block in front of the blind, but fear your God. I am the LORD."

15 "Do not pervert justice; do not show partiality to the poor or favoritism to the great, but judge your neighbor fairly."

16 "Do not go about spreading slander among your people."

"Do not do anything that endangers your neighbor's life. I am the LORD."

17 "Do not hate your brother in your heart. Rebuke your neighbor frankly so you will not share in his guilt."

18 "Do not seek revenge or bear a grudge against one of your people, but love your neighbor as yourself. I am the LORD."

19 "Keep my decrees."

"Do not mate different kinds of animals."

"Do not plant your field with two kinds of seed."

"Do not wear clothing woven of two kinds of material."

26 "Do not practice divination or sorcery."

28 "Do not cut your bodies for the dead or put tattoo marks on yourselves. I am the LORD."

29 "Do not degrade your daughter by making her a prostitute, or the land will turn to prostitution and be filled with wickedness."

30 "Observe my Sabbaths and have reverence for my sanctuary. I am the LORD."

31 "Do not turn to mediums or seek out spiritualists, for you will be defiled by them. I am the LORD your God."

32 "Rise in the presence of the aged, show respect for the elderly and revere."

There are more of these, so read your holy books. Just from this list above, it is obvious that we have changed much of what God has asked us to do on His Earth. I can only say, thank God for the covenant with Noah, or we might be treading water.

You are not a spiritualist or medium if you are **only** communicating with God, Jesus, Mary or the Angels. They are not considered humans that have died. They are alive and you can talk to these souls without offending God. You are not allowed to initiate contact with any other spirits, yourself or through someone else for the purpose of calling their spirit to you.

Giotto di Bondone 1276-1337 Public Domain

Prayer to Lose Weight

I ask for love so all can see,
No more of me than is need be.
For now is God my eternity,
And less of me than ever be.

More love from He is food to me,
More drink in me, less cavity.
I choose for none, in place of three
Stead more is give away with me.

So this I ask Our Savior be,
Give strength in character of me;
So in my test away from He,
I live in grace, but happily.

So now I say unto you I see
This God has made me sane;
For now I choose the right for me
Instead of that of more unseen.

Bless me God away of Thee,
For now this be my try,
In food or eat with only Thee,
By You I see my pride.

To live our life in such a mess,
When none should have this sense;
Good judgment give us now today,
For ever hold our place.

Lastly, I want to ask that no matter what comes of this plan, that any who meet me, allow me to be humble in God's eyes and yours. God has been working very hard on me to try to teach me humility before sending me into the world. I have been struggling with this since day one. I pray for God's help, to take no pride in anything I do, because it is only through God that I have done anything. If good comes of what happens, I ask you to give all praise of it to God. If anything I can do or help you with, gives you what you need, give only God your thanks. Please, please do not thank me for what Jesus Christ does; I would not want to insult Him.

My real joy is in watching God work. You may see me smile up to Him when I am overwhelmed at His love, or when I see His humor come out. I have been in awe of Our God since I started to hear His words and realized how loving He truly is. When I was young, my church put the fear of God into me; and believe me I did fear Him. I feared Him so much that I was afraid to talk to Him. So knowing God in such a loving manner now is a great surprise to me, and one I cherish with all my heart. God does expect a lot of us, but is patient and clever in His teaching, and to be honest, I find His manner most interesting and just.

I have not found changing my life to be an easy road, but once I discovered the love that God has for us, and the pain He has endured all these years for us, I had more than enough reason to want to change my life. Thanks to Our Blessed LORD holding my hand through these changes, I have learned to give thought to every instance when my tempter or my selfishness has brought me to sin against God. After you give yourself a few days to cool down about what you didn't get from God, that you thought you deserved, you can think clearly about why God didn't give you what you prayed for. Know that God only gives what will be good for you in your relationship to His will for you.

So in a sense, when God forbids that you get something from Him or do something in life that you want to do, it is for your eternal life with Him that this decision is made. God does not take your life as insignificantly as you do. Every aspect of your life is important to Him, down to the minute details. God does not want you to spend even one moment of your life giving Satan a chance to take you away from your place in Heaven. So His rules for you appear harsh, because of the many years we have been bending them to suit our will. But God sees all He has given us, as a way for us to come home to Him, because of His great love for us. God knows that in order to get to Heaven, we have to prove our worth here on Earth. If you give in to the desires of Earth that Satan puts before you, to hurt God, then you are not proving to God that you think your life is worth His love and trust, and even if you say the words, "God, I love you", you are not living up to those words, and they mean nothing without living the truth of them.

Just like God is holding my hand, He is waiting to hold yours. He is waiting to personally guide you through this life to a better one in Heaven. Simply give this a chance.

(This is a Baptism Poem or Prayer)

Arise sweet man, away from sin;
He comes for you in life begin,
To toil His way in journey fierce,
He saves us all of even worse.
A sprinkle of water,
A pat to crown,
Is all it takes for thee unfound.

William Adophe 1825-1905 Public Domain

—Carol—question
"Jesus, have You anything else You want me to know?"

—Jesus—answer
"This. I have come for you in spirit of love for man; now man should come for Me, with spirit of love of God. This I wish all to know;

> **God has asked Our child for message of this given**
> **for world peace with God, not peace of world.**
> **This is God's plan; world peace with God."**

—Carol—question
"Jesus, when You were on Earth, did You bear the pain of our sins during the time You were growing up?"

—Jesus—answer
"I left all pain in God's hands until the crucifixion; then all pain came unto Me; for My end to sin of mankind was excruciating, inside as well as physical. None have asked Me this question, now all will know how much I suffered for them."

—Carol

> *"Jesus, I am sorry for myself and that of the whole world,*
> *from the beginning of man."*

> *"Why, why did You?*
> *What is it about mankind's relationship with God that*
> *You would die so horridly and in so much pain to save us?*
> *We seem so ordinary for You to bless us in such a huge way."*

—Jesus—answer
"This is what you need to know about your relationship with God. Man is all there is that gives God His answer to His existence. Without mankind, God only exists of Us in Heaven. For God this did not give enough honor for making Earth, without something showing honor to God for His Divine effort toward its creation, makes the creation useless and God does nothing that has not cause with effect given back.

"All Our effort of keeping mankind alive and giving love of Us is effect of creation, with honor for God. This mankind should understand of Us.

"We have created your beings, as proof that God exists."

224

"This battle with Satan is just Our way of showing Lucifer that without God, he does not exist. Nothing will exist if mankind does not honor God. Carol, My daughter in pain, you have given your will for Us to give all Earth these answers. I know you are thinking that God is using you and all mankind to give only honor of Him. But Our love for you is more strong than Our desire for this honor. So in this you must not hesitate to show Us love also.

"No one understands Our Father in Heaven. He created Earth with so much passion of soul; that for God, Earth, was His most honored gift from His being. So when His mankind and Angels gave Him reason to wish against it; He was devastated of this, His most cherished pleasure. Now you know your answer.

"God wishes man know how much He has done to give them His love and protection; while with His great love, He waits for them to give Him back this love and honor His soul needs. Our God is Holy above all else. This Holiness prevents His life end all pain of what is given Him. So He sent Me, to heal His soul with a great sacrifice of pain and humility towards His honor. I gave My life for you, wholeheartedly to God, for I knew His great suffering pain, of need this honor done for He, who is all there is to all in life. Carol, please don't fail to give Us your love above all."

—Carol

"Jesus I feel like I am making You hurt all over again."

—Jesus

"I give this of your will for know why your Father has given His children so much. He is a patient soul, who has been willing to love even the worst of man, to receive love back and show His way of existence is above all else known of Earth beings. Our home is glorious child; it is and has more honor and praise of God, than any of Earth could understand or know about. Heaven is honor with pride, for a God who brings eternal light to so many souls who exist there. They give God love for each one on Earth that refuses to give honor of His love over them. This is Our way of surviving amongst evil-struck humans, who bring glory only to themselves while here of Earth, then never more allowed with God's home above.

"You must know this daughter, that We wait of the day, We will give honor again to God through showing Our children His love around them, and knowing that day will focus all your love towards Our LORD's asked question, for peace to His soul.

"Yes child, God created man to look like His son to make His son welcome of Earth. But God put His will for their good life, into each child He created, in hope of getting good will of His soul returned from them. Now as this Earth nears a new way of living with God; We of Heaven are giving every child on Earth, Our most precious child (me) to help them survive of Our Earth show, this coming year. Many on Earth will fear what God has in store for their view, each time Our Carol approaches a new nation problem.

"Carol, God needs your undivided attention and love during your 12 years of praise toward His plan. Because many unusual events will occur that will bring people closer to God and will make them know He exists around them solely of love for trust out toward He, will end some of what is planned in those times."

—Carol—question
"Are You saying that what happens will not stop until mankind
trusts God to stop it?"

—Jesus—answer
"This is Our answer; We will let Our daughter begin praise with hope of ending what is seen, then call upon God Father to all mankind, to end what is presented they."

—Carol—question
"Is this going to scare me also?"

—Jesus—answer
"You will know Us enough to trust We will give end when you ask of Us to do so. But do not end these too soon of asking Our will. For the longer they last, the greater gift you give to all on Earth for remembering power toward God alone."

—Carol—question
"You told Sr. Faustina to trust You completely and not anyone
on Earth. Do You ask this of me also?"

—Jesus—answer
"No, you will need to trust some who will be asking Our will for them. Give Me call if you doubt your ability to love them unconditionally, for I will give courage again for this end."

Luke 18—Jesus
The Parable of the Pharisee and the Tax Collector
9 To some who were confident of their own righteousness and looked down on everybody else, Jesus told this parable: 10 "Two men went up to the temple to

pray, one a Pharisee and the other a tax collector. 11 The Pharisee stood up and prayed about himself: 'God, I thank you that I am not like other men—robbers, evildoers, adulterers—or even like this tax collector. 12 I fast twice a week and give a tenth of all I get.'

13 "But the tax collector stood at a distance. He would not even look up to heaven, but beat his breast and said, 'God, have mercy on me, a sinner.'

14 "I tell you that this man, rather than the other, went home justified before God. For everyone who exalts himself will be humbled, and he who humbles himself will be exalted."

This is the "Our Father" or "The LORD's Prayer"

Our Father, Who art in Heaven,
hallowed be Thy Name.
Thy Kingdom come.
Thy will be done on Earth, as it is in Heaven.
Give us this day our daily bread
and forgive us our trespasses as we
forgive those who trespass against us;
and lead us not into temptation,
but deliver us from evil.
for thine is the kingdom,
and the power,
and the glory,
(and You are our love)
now and forever.
Amen.

"The LORD's Prayer" was given to the Apostles by Jesus when they asked how they should pray to God.

The Apostles, being human, remembered the words of Jesus in their own way. So in the Bible, the version of St. Luke (XI, 2-4), and St. Matthew (VI, 9-15) are slightly different. And the original translations from Aramaic to English read also a bit different from the prayer above, but they all have the same meaning.

"The LORD's Prayer"

Our Father

*We give God a child-like love and respect as our source of life,
body and soul.*

Who art in Heaven,

*We acknowledge that God is not human among us, but a divine spirit in a place we
perceive as holy, where only goodness and beauty exists.*

hallowed be Thy Name.

*We give God reverence and worship Him and a promise to only
use the name of God as it befits His Holy Spirit.*

Thy Kingdom come.

*We are saying that we believe that God will take us to be with Him in Heaven (our
home) and that our souls are already a part of God,
our Heavenly Father.*

Thy will be done on Earth, as it is in Heaven.

*We acknowledge that only God's will is important to us,
and we let go of our pride and promise to do His will.*

Give us this day our daily bread

*We ask God to help us through our day; this prayer is to be said each day. As in the
message from the Angel, God wants us to devote our daily activities to Him out of love
for Him and ask Him to give us what we need to achieve the outcome we ask Him to
provide for us.*

and forgive us our trespasses as we
forgive those who trespass against us;

*Here we are asking God to forgive us in the same manner as we
forgive others. Saying this, also reminds us that Our Father in Heaven expects us to
forgive others as He forgives us. This gives you a moment to think about your actions,
and how you responded to others.*

The Angels speak to me a lot about 'God's Way' and how important
it is for people to live in God's Way. (Meaning according to God's will
and in the manner in which God would act.) So if we are not acting in this
manner, then we have something to ask forgiveness for.

If we choose not to forgive others (remember we are all a part of God.
Our souls are like DNA of God. He is our Father by this type of spiritual
DNA) then we are in turn saying we will not forgive God's child, or
our brother/sister. But in this passage of the Our Father, we say to God
forgive me in the way I forgive my brother.

and lead us not into temptation,

*We ask God to direct our lives and lead us away from all that
would harm our relationship with Him and make our lives harder
and our afterlife in Heaven, impossible.*

but deliver us from evil.

*We ask God to keep Satan and the fallen angels away from us. (All that is evil that
tempts us everyday on Earth.) We acknowledge here that God is the safe haven and the
only one who can keep evil from us. This is the line that will save the Earth, as well as
give you much peace.*

for thine is the kingdom,
and the power,
and the glory,
(and You are our love)
now and forever.

*We acknowledge that God is the king and has the power over us,
His servants. To God, belongs the glory and honor and praise,
because without Him, we cannot exist, nor can our Earth,*

which He is asking us, His servants to protect with Him today.
He is our love only. No other is love.

Amen.

Saying Amen is like saying I have asked and God will respond and
I acknowledge that fact and believe it.
God told us, ask and you shall receive.
Please notice the use of the word (us).
We say this prayer to God for not only ourselves,
but for all mankind.

Close your eyes, and bow your head; say this prayer slowly and without pride of self. Remember you are petitioning your creator for His help. Would you want someone to ask you for help by rattling off words they memorized, without feeling or emotion?

After you say this prayer, sit quietly, keep your eyes closed and think of God. Let God give you His will, through images in your mind.

"The LORD's Prayer" in 1438 languages can be found at this website.
http://www.christusrex.org/www1/pater/index.html

St. Matthew 6:9-13
9 "This, then, is how you should pray:
"'Our Father in heaven,
hallowed be your name,
10 your kingdom come,
your will be done
on Earth as it is in heaven.
11 Give us today our daily bread.
12 Forgive us our debts,
as we also have forgiven our debtors.
13 And lead us not into temptation,
but deliver us from the evil one.'

14 For if you forgive men when they sin against you,
your heavenly Father will also forgive you.
15 But if you do not forgive men their sins,
your Father will not forgive your sins.

Unknown Artist, Public Domain

The LORD's Prayer

St. Luke 11:1-4

1 One day Jesus was praying in a certain place. When he finished, one of his
disciples said to him, "LORD, teach us to pray,
just as John taught his disciples."

2 He said to them, "When you pray, say:

**"'Father,
hallowed be your name,
your kingdom come.
3 Give us each day our daily bread.
4 Forgive us our sins,
for we also forgive everyone who sins against us.
And lead us not into temptation.'"**

5 Then he said to them, "Suppose one of you has a friend, and he goes to him
at midnight and says, 'Friend, lend me three loaves of bread, 6 because a friend
of mine on a journey has come to me, and I have nothing to set before him.'

7 "Then the one inside answers, 'Don't bother me.
The door is already locked, and my children are with me in bed. I can't get up
and give you anything.' 8 I tell you, though he will not get up and give him the
bread because he is his friend,
yet because of the man's boldness he will get up and
give him as much as he needs.

9 "So I say to you: Ask and it will be given to you; seek and you will find;
knock and the door will be opened to you.
10 For everyone who asks receives; he who seeks finds;
and to him who knocks, the door will be opened.

Psalm 66 For the director of music. A song. A psalm.
1 Shout with joy to God, all the Earth!
2 Sing the glory of his name;
make his praise glorious!
3 Say to God, "How awesome are your deeds!
So great is your power
that your enemies cringe before you.
4 All the earth bows down to you;
they sing praise to you,
they sing praise to your name."
Selah

5 Come and see what God has done,
how awesome his works in man's behalf!
6 He turned the sea into dry land,
they passed through the waters on foot—
come, let us rejoice in him.
7 He rules forever by his power,
his eyes watch the nations—
let not the rebellious rise up against him.
Selah

8 Praise our God, O peoples,
let the sound of his praise be heard;
9 he has preserved our lives
and kept our feet from slipping.
10 For you, O God, tested us;
you refined us like silver.
11 You brought us into prison
and laid burdens on our backs.
12 You let men ride over our heads;
we went through fire and water,
but you brought us to a place of abundance.
13 I will come to your temple with burnt offerings
and fulfill my vows to you-
14 vows my lips promised and my mouth spoke
when I was in trouble.
15 I will sacrifice fat animals to you
and an offering of rams;
I will offer bulls and goats.
Selah

16 Come and listen, all you who fear God;
let me tell you what he has done for me.
17 I cried out to him with my mouth;
his praise was on my tongue.
18 If I had cherished sin in my heart,
the LORD would not have listened;
19 but God has surely listened
and heard my voice in prayer.
20 Praise be to God,
who has not rejected my prayer
or withheld his love from me!

Guido Remi 1575-1642 Public Domain

To put this into **Perspective** for you,

you are not being asked to do anything all that difficult.

Throughout history God has sent Angels to give us messages about what we are supposed to do for Him. The Bible is full of stories about people who were told to do some very mind-boggling things for God. They obeyed. I am sure Abram's wife's pregnant slave Hagar was less than thrilled to be told to return to her mistress after being used and abused by Abram and his wife; but Hagar was part of God's plan. You are also not being asked to build a boat like Noah.

But you are simply being asked to pray and give God your day's work because you love Him. To watch how people you trust are using your trust, and to act like you carry God within you. You are not 86 years old and being asked to bring a country of people through a desert for forty years and through a river to another location, like Moses did. Can you imagine being over 100 years old and climbing a mountain, no food or drink, no bed to rest on for 40 days and then carrying heavy tablets of stone down to a bunch of people who then grumble about the laws you are bringing to them.

It is my understanding that when Lucifer rebelled against God, a third of the Angels sided with him. God banded all of them from Heaven. So who knows how many a third of the Angels really is. This is what you are up against everyday. Don't you want God to help you? You don't even know what you are fighting, but God does. So if God sends Angels, and comes through me to give you His plan, are you going to disregard His help? Do you think you have a better plan? I'm 58 years old, I've seen your plans; and God is much older and He has seen your plans also.

Many people around the world have been praying to God to change the wrongs being done on Earth. God has heard our prayers and has responded with this plan. There is no other way to combat evil, than to come together in love with Our Father. That's it, that's the only way. You can't shoot or bomb the invisible. You simply can't capture or kill Satan.

We have to give our brothers and sisters credit for trying hard to change the effects of corrupt behavior. Some work through the churches and organizations to bring help to those who have been victimized by evil means and left to die or suffer. Some try to use government to change the evil around the world. Some use war to try to right the wrongs done. Others call action through holy wars to try to bring God back to those who ignore Him and insult the rest of us with their wicked behavior. All of this is our attempt to change what Satan has done to us. We fight each other, or accuse each other of wrongs that Satan is responsible for. I give each of these people my love, for their efforts to fight our unseen enemy in whatever means our human mind can bring forth.

But God in His goodness and mercy has watched us struggle to find the answer to fighting these wrongs. He knows we don't understand that to fight each other is not going to end this evil around the world. In fact, it will increase the problem. Helping the victim is commendable and needed, but will not stop the cause of their injuries. We all want to see our world change for the better.

Even those who are given incorrect knowledge about cause for justice are doing their best to make some kind of change that will help those who are close to them live a better life. My heart goes out to them the most. We are all desperate to help those we love to stop hurting in so many ways. Some to the point of giving up their own life for a cause greater than they. My heart aches for these people because in their desperation for their loved ones; they have been fooled by Satan into thinking that killing is justified by God. I pray for God's mercy for all who have killed others this way, and I ask that the rest of you find a way to forgive those who are being overtaken by these invisible evil ones, who have been giving mankind all the wrong answers as to how to change Earth. I also ask those who are involved in this massacre of human life to find a way to forgive the wrong done by those who you find offensive, because like yourselves, Satan has brought their good hearts into these actions.

Our God, the one God who created all of us on Earth, has mercifully given us the answer that is going to make life worth living. God wants us to get rid of the one source that is behind every problem of mankind. God says that to rid Earth of Satan, we have to stop accusing each other, stop fighting each other, and stop taking advantage of each other. We also need to stop thinking of ourselves and our will for this life. We do have to find God in each other, find love for each other, and find a way to ask Our Father to come to live with us on Earth *through His will for us.*

Once we bring God to Earth by shear will power towards this end and stand together; God with man, one man with another; one nation with another; then we send Satan from Earth by the power of God.

God fights with the power of love alone.
When you are God; your sword shines with the light of love,
your edge is sharpened with the word of truth.

In the Bible it is written that God's sword comes out of His mouth. This is stated because one word of truth from God will cut deeper and surer than any weapon made. One word from God will end a life eternally. No other has that kind of power, because no other has that kind of truth and the knowledge to back it up. Only God who created everything has the power and will to end everything. He who is, who was and who is to come.

What is the one reason that God has not struck down Satan? Why is Satan still on Earth after all these years of tormenting God's children and hurting God? Think about it. If we are hurt and angry about what is happening to us because of Satan, can you imagine how much more in pain God is over his actions?

God is all holy, and can not see even evil without love. This means that God has a way to create love from every evil done. God uses Satan to bring us love. He is using Satan again in this plan to bring us love.

We can choose to live this plan and for once, snub our noses at Satan the way he has always done to us, or we can go on letting Satan take away the love God is offering.

God did not take Satan from Earth because He is waiting for us to give our freewill up and ask Him to help us. This way is the only way He can prove to Satan once and for all, just who has all the power and who has all our love.

When this happens and it will, this Earth will completely change. Within the next twelve years, everything about the way we live will change. Are you going to be ready for this?

Are you in a business that will not be accepted by God? What do you plan on doing the day after Jesus, the son of God shows up on Earth? Do you know anything about inventing kneelers? A lot of them will be needed in the upcoming years. I am sure if you give it some thought, you will realize a whole new set of industries will be needed to accommodate a world with God foremost in our minds.

I for one will be looking forward to seeing how minds cleaned of evil thoughts and united with the will of God can invent and create things far beyond anyone's present imagination. With no disease or disasters or wars to put our efforts into, we can be free to create with God, a world where liking each other and loving each other will . . . I am so excited I can't even think of the right words. My mind is just dancing.

. . . .

Here is an eye-opening discovery I made while learning these lessons from God.

1. God does not see anything without love.
2. We are told to forgive our enemies.
3. Satan and the fallen angels are our enemies.
4. Pray for your enemies so that they return to God.

—The Holy Spirit
"My end is without error. I do not curse of this evil one, for he (Lucifer) is Mine. I am without sin of heart . . . for evil only exists for Earth."

If we are to follow God's plan, then we need to do the same thing all Heaven is doing; pray for the fallen angels and Lucifer to find a way back to the love of God. When you are being tormented by these spirits, pray for them, not just so they leave you alone, but for them to leave all Earth and go back to God. We were told God is waiting for them, to forgive them the same way He is waiting for us.

We are all God's creation. God loves all no matter what you have done, and as long as you love Him, you will not be condemned. God sent Lucifer from Heaven because he put himself and his pleasures before God, and he should have known better than to test God. But our Holy God does not see these fallen angels or us, outside of His love for us.

God has been patiently waiting all these years for them and us to have a change of heart. He has been waiting for us to wake up to what is being done to us, and begin to make the changes needed to rid Earth of evil. Because our God is all love, and only love, the only plan He could give all of us, is a plan of prayer, love and kindness. So He gave us the only plan that can work for all mankind as well as the fallen angels, God's other lost sheep.

God told us, do what you most hate. So if you hate praying for Satan; do it. If you hate being good; do it. We are all bringing huge amounts of pain to God, our Father, our Creator, our only means of love. So if God asks for this plan to be followed to ease the pain He has endured since before mankind, then just do it. How can you bear knowing God is in such pain and sorrow over us? How can you say the words "Peace of God be with you"; if you know God is not at peace?

I am telling you that when God told me how much pain He was in, I could not bear the emotion that overwhelmed me because of the sorrow He endures for love of us. I know that not one person on Earth could feel the pain He shared with me that day and not want to do everything humanly possible to relieve that pain for God and for Jesus Christ who suffered untold amounts for us. Until now, we just did not have the least bit of knowledge about this side of God. We think of God as powerful, so never think that our small sins could hurt Him so much. But each one . . . each one, is His pain. Now multiply that by all the humans and fallen angels and think about how much of that you would be able to withstand for the sake of mankind.

This plan is our chance to give God peace. Can you imagine what our Father would give to us in return? This is God . . . who can do anything. Anything but ease His own pain, because love for Lucifer and the fallen angels means He has to give them the same consideration He gives us. He does not play favorites. So He can't go against His own truth to free us of this evil. The only way out, is for us to do it through love and trust in God. Any other plan would only increase God's pain.

Then Lucifer will know we choose God, and our prayer for the evil ones will show them that we want them to choose God with us. **Love your enemy.**

So all those Bible stories that we thought referred to only those on Earth, were actually meant to bring us to this conclusion, so that God could have some peace.

Pray hard for those who will not see this truth. Because of you, the others will be saved.

This is a Shortened Version, for a Quick Reference.

First Thing, Every Morning

—**Pray "The LORD's Prayer" slowly**
—Think about the meaning of the words as you say them.
—Give God your freewill and ask for His will for you as you say the words (Thy will be done on Earth, as it is in Heaven) this will do two things, One, it will get your heart in touch with God's Divine Soul's desire of what He likes about you. These are your talents, gifts and strengths.

Two, God is constantly doing things that concern your life and His purpose for you. Giving love to God in this manner opens up your mind to those thoughts and will replace the thoughts you have of what you think you would or should be doing.

—**God's words**
"We unite with Almighty God once our soul brings thoughts of love and hope up to Our LORD God Almighty. He then graces us with loves light upon our hearts, so that in union with His powerful soul; we share in His strength-giving ability to create for our lives what God intended happening with Him.

"This is called, **'Satisfactory Blessing'**.
A much-intended pleasure with God."

This is a little prayer God gave me that is perfect for asking for the will of God. This prayer can be said all day long when you need God's help.

**"Almighty God,
I will Thee give Your knowledge,
so that answers come suddenly;
for knowing Thy will,
can enable the right course of this day."**

This is a Shortened Version, for a Quick Reference

After you say The Lord's Prayer, **tell God that you are giving Him all the work you are doing that single day—as love for Him.** (Do not give the things you do for your parents and family or your friends or people you do favors for, they are not your work, you do those things to show honor and respect to them, and out of love for them.)

Give only chores you do at home that need to be done, and also the work you do that you get paid to do. All this work is love for God no matter how small the job is. You can also give study and anything you do that teaches you lessons.

God waits quietly until we give love and trust to Him, then we are in Heaven's thoughts of us; this is why we ask Our God before hand when we do our work. For only through God should we honor others with our labors, for in God is our greatest effort available to this.

<table>
<tr><td>**This Is Essential**</td><td>—Think only about this one day's work. Do not think past the day you are in. Think over all the work you know you have to do that day and do not extend your work to the next day even if you don't think you will finish it all that day. (Remember you will be doing this same thing again tomorrow, so you have no reason to think past one day) It makes today important.</td></tr>
</table>

Then, ask God for the outcome you would like for the day. So if you have to meet with particularly nasty people that day, then ask God to make that meeting go in your favor. Or ask that the meeting be pleasant. If you have a lot to do that day, ask for a nice even flow to the day, so that you are not rushed one minute and have nothing to do the next. You can ask for whatever kind of day you want.

Then after you have asked God to bless you in this manner, just sit quietly and try to relax your mind. Because now that you asked; God has to adjust the entire universe and eternity to comply with your request. He will send thoughts and pictures into your head. (Like imagination)

—God's words
"Always give God the time needed when a thought comes into your head about His will of your day. For God has adjusted your

life of His desires and adjusts all eternity because you have asked His will for your day. Be still, silent to hear Our LORD's response, for God has given you this time of reflection, to bring His thoughts of will into picture within your mind. He gives you His grace so that you might picture His mind."

—Gods words
"Also, I give strength of will, to all who attempt my effort of them."

<table>
<tr><td>

Here Is the Hard Part

</td><td>

—God wants you to do your work in a way that shows honor to Him. You are to work to bring glory to God. This means once you give God your work, you have to put your best effort into it. And God will not let you offer your work to Him and then sit and feel bad about yourself or your life. You have to spend the day doing chores that are an appropriate gift to God, even if you don't feel like it.

</td></tr>
</table>

Also, while you go through your day that you offered to God, you can't tell any lies to anyone, or do things that will only benefit you when you know someone else is in need and you can do something about it. You can't say that is good enough when you don't want to put any more effort into something or it is for someone you don't like.

This is the reason you have to do your best. God gave all of us a different amount of ability. So, at the end of the day, God judges you on the ability He gave you.

—God's words
"After you serve God in this way, then rest your soul. Give thanks to God for His work towards the outcome you asked for." (I normally say another 'Our Father' and then just talk to God.)

—God's words
"Rest of soul refers to how you will **give God your thanksgiving for His labors on your behalf. You must kneel before God when you end your day.** This will show Almighty God that you have come in His presence out of graced gratitude, leaving your pride away. Our LORD sees your head bowed before His form, then says all is done in honor towards Himself."

At the End of the Day

—God's words

"God has to give His say about what you accomplished. Judge your ability of this project given to you (your work). For if God thinks it is unfinished of the knowledge he has given to you, then your honor towards Him is also not complete. So it is with His answer justly, that work is finished for us who are given His will for us."

—God's words

"**I am all there is.** This I say of Myself; for none other will give salvation of mankind. All belongs to Me; all praise of honor is Mine; only of Our way for mankind will honor toward Me, give them Us in Heaven. No life is more precious than a life within US. Our way of true power exist alone, without just course given you on Earth; for now on Earth is your reward if no thought is given toward Our love. **Save yourselves if you want Us around yourselves eternally.**"

If you think you can live this life without going to God, then God lets you. But once you have chosen that path, you will not get God's heavenly reward. After you say this prayer, sit quietly and wait. Let God show you His will for you, which He says will come in images into your mind.

Don't get discouraged if it takes you some time to begin to recognize God's will in your mind. I suggest you do this for at least 30 minutes each day, longer if you have the time.

Learning a new way to communicate with God is going to take a while for some people, but that is okay; we all need to move at our own pace. It takes some more time to relax and learn to accept God's will coming to you than it takes others. Don't worry about it; it will happen when you are ready to give up your control over your will.

I encourage you not to think about your day while you wait, because you don't want to be imagining your will for that day, and then, get confused when God is putting images into your mind. Be careful not to impose your will on God, and just expect He is going to give you what you are asking for. It does not work that way. You cannot ask God to do your will. The whole purpose of praying this way is to get from God, His purpose for your life one day at a time.

You might try one of these methods while you sit quietly and wait for Gods will:

— Read prayers that you don't know by heart, so that your mind does not wander to thoughts of your day.

— Read a holy book.

— Say prayers for people you don't know; the souls in Purgatory, the sick and dying around the world, the poor and homeless. Think about them and not about yourself. Pray as if you were they; you are the one in Purgatory waiting for help, you are about to die and think you can't ask for God because you have led an evil life, you are sick and too weak to pray for yourself, you are poor and have nothing to eat, you are homeless and tired and have no bed to rest in. Pray for all those who are being outsmarted by Satan and don't know it. We have a lot to pray for, so use your time waiting for a good purpose.

—God

"I say one thing more of this time: Give thought of God. Say, "Holy God we praise You for your look upon us Your children." Then simply kneel before the site of Our LORD Jesus as you contemplate His Holy ways He taught while here on Earth. These of Us are your guidelines and you need to remember Our way is most clear.""

—Carol, not knowing what to ask.
"Jesus?"

—Jesus—answer

"Yes you are in Our thoughts, for this is not your easiest chore of this life child. Telling mankind to give all they own of their life over to God through end with freewill is difficult choice for any who offer this. But most of God's children will understand how wonderful this small gesture of faith, with love to God can change everything about Earth, from that day forward in their life. Never fear Us, only try your best to please Us and We will do the rest."

—Carol
"Thank you, Jesus."

I have been asked about identifying the images from God. I normally explain it this way. The images come through your imagination, which is our only source for picturing what is in our mind. However, when you normally imagine something, you program what the picture will be. If you say to yourself, "I imagine a candle, and it is tapered with a flame burning brightly." Then in your mind's eye, this is what you see. You have told your mind what to expect and your mind provides the pictures you want.

When you get images from God, you will see them within your imagination the same way you see what you program. With one huge difference; you will not be programming them. Instead a picture will pop quickly into your mind as if someone just turned on the television. It is not something you expected to see because you were thinking about it. It is something that will fascinate you and delight you with a great surprise, like when you click the TV on and a picture appears that is totally unexpected. This is how you can tell if God is giving you His will for you.

If you are sitting, thinking about what you want to happen in your life and you get a picture, then it is from your own mind and you are trying to ask God to do your will.

Do whatever you can to keep yourself from programming your day, the way most people have been taught to do their entire life. This is a new beginning for you and your relationship with Our LORD.

Praise the LORD in your own words (I am told that pleases Him) or if you can't find the words you wish to use, you can do as I sometimes do and use the words from the bible in the *Book of Revelations*. These words are what the souls in Heaven say to praise God. These are souls who are with God; who are not waiting for judgment. These souls praise God eternally, because they see His greatness and understand how His love and justice works. They know that only God has the power of life and death, and who will receive punishment. They also know the love of God and the glory of Heaven and what it means to be able to be a part of God's plans.

God tells us that if we live in His way, we will be with Him in Heaven. I like to say these praises now in hopes that one day I will be blessed to say them in Heaven.

"Holy, holy, holy, is the LORD God Almighty,
who was and is and is to come."

You are worthy, Our LORD and God,
to receive glory and honor and power,
for you created all things,
and by your will they were created and have their being."

"Great and marvelous are your deeds,
Lord God Almighty.
Just and true are your ways,
King of the ages.
Who will not fear you, O Lord,
and bring glory to your name?
For you alone are holy.
All nations will come
and worship you,
for your righteous acts have been revealed."

"Hallelujah!
Salvation and glory and power belong to our God,
for true and just are his judgments ;

"Praise our God,
all you His servants,
you who fear him,
both small and great."

Come, LORD Jesus

By saying these prayers, you are thanking God in advance for saving Earth from Satan.

Asking God for His Will

We were all taught to pray to God for what we want, but Jesus taught us that God already knows what we want. In this book we are told by God that praying for self alone is evil. Why would it be evil?

We have a choice; ask God His plan for our life, or try to plan our own life. When God plans our life, His plan starts before conception and lasts throughout eternity. So God's plan for us and His will for us will never be the same plan we make. Our knowledge of life is what we see and are told. That being, what is on earth, and a promise of an afterlife, which most of us give little consideration because we are pretty much wrapped up in survival of this life.

That having been said is the reason we pray selfishly for the completion of our plan for this life. The first commandment of God tells us that it is a sin to put anything before God. So, if you plan your life, and never ask God what His plan is for you, then it is because Satan has convinced you that your will is important. That's a hard pill to swallow! Finding out that your whole life you followed the will of Satan while you prayed to God for what you want on earth. Is it no wonder God is in pain?

We kneel before God, asking Him to make our will, His will for us. Some people believe you can manifest anything into your life. If you will it hard enough . . . then God will give it to you. Guess who else is listening when we do this, with a big smile of satisfaction on his face? How many of us have asked God to overlook His Commandments and give us something that will surely make us or someone else break a commandment if we have our prayer to God answered.

The single person's prayer: "God please send me someone to have sex with." The married person's prayer: "God please get my husband that job where he travels a lot." The greedy person's prayer: "God please let me win this lottery." The guy that just paid for a negative advertising campaign against his opponent: "God help me to win this election." The guy fighting a case for pro abortion: "God help me to win this court case." "God if only you help me steal this one last car without getting caught." In your life, how many times have you heard people ask God for help with something illegal or immoral? How many times have you heard God thanked on award shows for help with songs and movies with stories and lyrics that slam down a number of the commandments. Do you really think it was God who helped with those? Or the other guy who was listening to those prayers and laughing at you for insulting God and hurting Him.

These same people, who pray selfishly, credit the will of God when their prayers get answered in their favor. A man who is having an affair, prays to God. "God if it's your will, find a way for me to leave my wife who doesn't understand me, and my children and be able to live with my girlfriend." A week later, his wife gets so angry at him for not coming home for two days, that she tells him to get out. The man says, "It's God's will that I leave my wife, I prayed and God found a way for me to do it. I never had to tell her that I wanted to leave. She gave me my freedom." Who are you kidding? I have heard many stories this silly, but they were all true.

And then there are the bargainers. "God if you do this for me . . . I will do . . ." Yes, that is impressive to God, and is also another lesson Jesus did not teach us. There is no parable about the man who bargained with God, and got his way. But there are stories about the Devil trying to make bargains with God and Jesus.

There are also people who think that no matter what happens, it's God's will. That's because God has all the power, His will is the only thing being done. However those people have overlooked the enormous number of evil spirits on earth, whose only job is to tempt mankind to do something stupid. Avoidance of asking the will of God is not doing the will of God. God only gives His will to those who ask Him for it. He will allow you free will to choose between Him and Satan. If you don't choose God, Satan just assumes you chose him, and will whisper his solutions for your life into your mind, your dreams, your every waking moment. You will go along thinking all is God's will. Every bad thing that happens to you will be credited to God. These are the people who in a disaster say, "It's God's will," or "God is punishing us for something. God tells us in this book that the prayers He answers are the ones that get you and/or someone else to heaven. If what you ask for is in HIS PLAN of your life or their life, then and only then will you get that prayer answered by God. He also tells us that if He is not answering your prayer, then Satan is giving you his answer to your problem. He tells us that for God, love for Him means obedience.

How many times in your life have you wondered why you were here? How many people have pondered this question? Yet few pondered a way to find out. We call them Saints. Those who asked the will of God, received His will for them. They unselfishly, and without pride of self, did what God gave them to do. Many of them suffered greatly at the hands of those who never asked God's will. God does not give his children easy lives. When He gives you his plan for your life, that plan involves a way to get you to heaven. Not only you, but He expects you to take along as many others as possible, because He knows not everyone will ask for His will. When I asked for His will, He told me to save as many as I can.

For me, if one person is saved because of what I do, then everything I have done is worth it to me. My greatest fear is letting the LORD down. It's better to let mankind find fault with you, than to let God find fault in your actions. It's better to struggle to do the will of God, than to sail through life on Satan's tail. God keeps telling me not to worry about pleasing Him, to just keep trying and He will do the rest for me.

The hard part of asking God for His will, is letting go of your pride, and letting go of your control. You are standing before God, your Father, and asking Him to use you in any way He chooses. You are looking into the soul of the being who holds your existence in His hands, and saying to Him, "I give you my life to do with as you please. I will do anything you ask of me."

Unlike getting married, God is not going to ask you to mow the lawn or have dinner on the table on time. God is going to ask you to do things that will get you to heaven. He is going to hand you your cross to bear. The only ones that get to heaven are the ones who are pure of heart; the ones who obey God. The ones, who know all the rules God gave Moses, were made by a being who could see into the future and is never wrong.

The nice part of getting God's will, is now you know. You don't have to wonder why you are on earth. You have a plan that will work, because God planned it and God makes good plans. God makes never-fail plans. What a relief that is. God is sending you out knowing you can't fail.

You have His plan, His knowledge and His ability to do this plan. All you have to do is walk through it. That doesn't mean the walk isn't going to be over cut glass or hot stones. It means that you will always know the direction to walk in. When you come to the path of cut glass, God will be there to wrap your feet. When you walk over hot stones, God will be there to pour cool water on them and heal the blisters. But at the end of the path, is the gate to Heaven. Doing God's will is the direct path to Heaven. This book teaches us how to learn God's will.

I asked Jesus why he prayed to God selfishly before He died. The bible said He asked God to take the cup from Him, but still He said, Thy will be done. And on the cross, He said to God, "My God, My God, why have You forsaken Me?" This is the answer Jesus gave me.

—Jesus
"I say this of using Our will. When I prayed of My Father at Gethsemane, I did not ask Our Heavenly Father to take His will from Me. I only prayed for support of Our Father to carry out His command of peace for His divine being. With no

thought given to ending what was begun of Us in Heaven. My followers, yes, did pray that God take away this cup of My end with earth. They who saw My blood pour from My skin believed My fear great. But My love is greater than humankind knows of Me; therefore, blind of this, they assumed fear in Me. And this is what was written about that night.

"On the cross, I asked My Heavenly Father to give Me love while mankind crucified Me. And in My excruciating pain with all man's sins of My being, God left these only in My hands for that was My greatest sacrifice to He who was before all beings existed. To give His son His pain as well as His pain from these who will follow Me. I save all because all was given Me this moment of time. This is when God hath forsaken Me. So that I with all His pain could accept fully your lives and those who passed before you."

—*Carol*

"I guess that was the only way to relieve God's pain; to take it all from Him."

—**Jesus**

"Yes child that is why I lived and died. For that one moment, when I would love the Father more than life; God allowed Me this great affection to His being. When I tell you that I gave this to My Father in Heaven whole heartedly, I was telling truth only.

"God does no evil towards prayer for self. (Jesus was referring to himself as God)
    Teach all how to give for God and pray for His will of them."

Let me just say this now. When I am before God to pray or listen to Him, the outpour of love from God is so strong for me and for all mankind that He is coming to me to talk about, that it is overwhelming to me. I know most people think of God as being so far away, up in Heaven, but when you pray to God, His soul is with you. You are kneeling in front of a King and the most powerful being that is. He is so powerful that when you call to Him, He has the power to come to you immediately without fail. Say His name and know He is with you. So because He is there with you, give Him all respect and reverence. Say the words of the Lord's Prayer as if you were speaking to the one who created all things from nothing. Say the words as if you were being consumed by His love for you, as you talk to Him; because you are. Say the words as if you are a child asking his beloved Father to help him, and tell God how much He is loved by you. Say, "Father, I love you." Ask God to forgive you for ignoring His needs of your love to Him by never asking His will of your life. Then ask God to bless you with the courage to ask for His will. It takes great courage to let go of your life and ask God unknowing of what He will answer, what His will is for your life. Because once you know, you will feel compelled to do as God asks of you. All who have asked God's will, struggled and suffered to do what God asked. And all who have asked God's will found out how much love God has for them. God always gives His ability and courage and strength and knowledge when He gives His will. To know God's will is the beginning of knowing who God truly is and so doing His will prepares you for meeting Him soul to soul.

. . . .

I will try to answer as many questions on my website as possible. Reading what others have tried or are having problems with may help. I will personally answer letters or e-mails if God feels you are on the wrong track and need His help. Remember this one thing; one method will not work for everyone. So don't get discouraged if what someone else is having success with, is not working for you. God will find a way for you to be successful as well.

If you are having difficult, you might also try to read 'Divine Mercy Diary' by St. Faustina. In her diary she explains some of the difficulties she had, and also you will find the Divine Mercy Chaplet, which is a wonderful way to help each other and give unconditional love that God talks about in this book.

I wanted to give all of us a reminder to say "The LORD's Prayer" in the morning, so I asked God to give us the perfect words of inspiration.

"Lord God is here for you."

"Have you given Me today's work, for which I have said is love for Me?

Have I not your love?"

Graphic Art by **Carol Aubuchon © 2007**

If you would like a copy of this, visit our website at:
www.Godsholyplan.com for products with this image.
Or *GodsHolyPlan@gmail.com*
for a free color copy sent to your e-mail.

	Times to Pray
This is your schedule to pray for our Earth. At any of these times, say "The LORD's Prayer;" ask God to save us from the coming of David.	7:00 AM
	8:00 AM
	9:00 AM
	1:00 PM
Three times a day pick one of these hours to pray with the rest of the world against evil being done during work hours.	2:00 PM
	3:00 PM
	5:00 PM
	6:00 PM
	7:00 PM

ALL OF US, PRAYING TOGETHER, WILL TAKE SATAN OFF THIS EARTH AND GIVE OUR GOD PEACE FOR THE FIRST TIME SINCE ADAM AND EVE.

I thought you might like to know God's answers to some of the questions I have been privileged to ask during my morning prayers. These are in no particular order.

"Are there different places in Heaven?"

"There are many. Our LORD gives many His site. Others His name for them is holier for they have given He, their all. Some without wrong but no build rapport with He, have place given of those who weep for His way in life."

. . . .

"Do we recognize each other in Heaven?"

"His name of our lips has more recognition, for they who have seen He. The rest that seem of Earth so important is now erased of us; for God's place with us has consumed every being that enters kingdom of LORD Holy Almighty."

. . . .

"At the end, will physical bodies rise to God or physical appearance in spiritual form be all that is allowed?"

"All corpses left will have an awakening; but those pieces of dirt are left as dirt. God requires only forms silk with white." (Spirits)

. . . .

"Has anyone ever died, and then come back to Earth like so many have claimed to have done?"

"Never has man come with LORD God; then send of Earth more. God has no involvement this manner, but many have believed this happened, because they wish Us more of them, but can't find answers along their way. For this reason, they choose imagine Us, when Earth accident of operation fails or brings drug induced hallucinations with answers based in further mind deep conscience of Our way."

. . . .

"Does the soul have a form?"

"Soul is God's plan to give life for human beings. Soul has only energy forces and gives God's energy through knowledge with Me. Also, I give My love of all Earth through this soul force.

"This is more information involved regarding Our will of your end. When man dies of body, soul is sent of Me with question of judgment pending its reward of Us. Should We decide this soul is not worthy yet for Heaven, soul gets sent with other souls holding, to wait of those from Earth who offer self-love toward them and give them enough reward toward their evil means done, to warrant grace with God's soul. This We call, **"Redemption of mankind through giving love"**.

"Only souls soft of love over peace with Me, get into home for pure. All others wait for those still alive, to bring them redemption of their sins against My way for them.

"Blessing come of both who participate in this love source. You give love for another's force of Me; then I consider it love for Me. This gives great redemption favor with God Almighty of Heaven. For only those giving this manner, know unconditional love for their mankind as well as God. All others simply offer prayer of self-love only. This sort of love is offensive brought before Me. For love over self forbids love towards God to come first; and this I give my first foremost commandment.

"Love thy friends of Earth over self, and love my poor souls lost before love with Me exists."

"What about love thyself first as you told me in the message?"

"This of Us is different means. When you love self first in this case, it means to give your soul's grace to God before you love all else on Earth. When you have done that, then you are free to love your neighbor and take care of Our poor souls, because you do it then as a way to obey the will of God."

> We need to go to God and ask Him, "Who do you want me to pray for today? Or you can say before you prayer, "God this prayer is for the soul you choose." Try to remember that God knows everything and all your thoughts, so He already knows your personal suffering. You don't have to keep reminding Him that you want things for yourself. Let your friends pray for you; you pray for them.

· ·

"True Earth consists of body persons, Angel souls, evil souls, lost spirits who roam, close enactment spirits who perish with body until I wake them; they stay encased of the grave until ground above moves aside to let them free. They do not realize ground not holding them, so stay put. Also many Angels walk like human beings, in case site of them should remove doubt, when asked help for Us."

> Here is another very good reason to love each other and strangers. You never know if someone you are talking to is an Angel of God.

. . . .

"Are Angels souls with spirits?"

"Angels are souls without spirits; but show themselves of every means through power given of Us. In Heaven, Angels are light force of soul, also beautiful color beings; given love for all Universe. On Earth, any means needed; requires many illusions given."

"Have Angels appeared on Earth with wings?"

"They appear all ways, given of Us. For mankind needs knowledge they understand to know these being are around them for purpose reported by God of them."

. . . .

"If souls have no form and the Bible said there will be gnashing of teeth in hell; then am I correct in thinking that this is an expression used to help us understand a feeling of frustration and despair, rather than a reality of what will happen?"

"Yes, We welcome your insight given this means. Bible is written of stories to make you understand realm of delusions you live in. Most of Earth will not want to know truth of this; for it is not understandable in your eyes and ears for you to reason why God chooses this means of Earth to do His will. But mankind is great imagination base person, so I give them food for their imaging of Us.

"Some of Earth will perish without ever knowing life around them. Others will see I put more than dirt at their feet and more than air in their space, and also others among them to spend time with them until I am ready to bring them of Me."

"God, you told me all the stories of the Bible are true?"

"All are true as truth is understood by mankind. But delusion exists around you, so if I say truth as I know, without course given you changed; then true statements would frighten Our children, and this is not purpose of Our LORD. Teaching love and trust is primary of Us always."

> I want to say something here to ease your minds about Earth being a delusion. Unfortunately, God has not given me any more information about this than that of which you are reading. I promise if more comes for me, I will share it with all Earth. In the meantime I believe God feels we all have to adjust to what has been given us.

. . . .

"Was it a great pleasure to create the world?"

"My soul offers so much of Me that giving this for many has given Us Our most honest joy. All I created I love. All I see is good of Me to see. All hope of this gives pleasure toward My life everlasting."

. . . .

"Will there be any more world wars?"

"None of Us is given this means of destroy My planet. I will thee say of this when asked this question. My Earth is holy of Us on high, so none below should think to destroy part for self-indulgence sake.

"I say one thing child; all is good of your heart toward this land. So give Our love to as many color race and creed of any as will come for Us, through your planned involvement toward Us. We will encourage those who see Us in you, to come follow along and encourage others to look of Us and you. Yes, you will travel all over this world, in Our names and give Our words of love to save all for Heaven."

. . . .

"This plan is not going to make all see its reward is it?"

"All have need but most will panic at thoughts based on ridding the Earth made evil. I want as many saved that can be saved. This pleases Me/God."

. . . .

"Will you give people reason that you are changing church laws?"

"Yes, I change only laws that have altered My Commandments, for they are giving Me sadness and offending Me. This is not done to make authorities appear unknowledgeable; it is done to help them rectify areas that have been altered, to appease their congregations.

"All appeasement should be only of Me and for Me. All adjustments are in My favor only. So these laws of church, I must adjust to reflect what I agree to uphold in Heaven. Earth will not be able to adjust only that bound of Us."

. . . .

"What about terrorism?"

"I say one thing about this; evil dwells deep of this means. All in Heaven bless Our souls who find horror in daily life from those who victimize them for the sake of build power over them. I did not teach My souls this form of brutality to convince others of your right. I give love of them for good of soul and proper manner in form.

"But those who say My name when touching others of terror means do Me injustice in their heart and soul, and I will punish this means and send them into poverty and mourning, for bringing such destruction for those whose lives become inflamed in hope of peace; but get torn to bits by soldiers dressed of evil colors, and battle underground as if hiding their evil-doing from Me, who can see them no matter where they hide.

"When one is right and just, all is done in the open to be judged as honest of heart. When only done in private means and underhanded tactics used, then all is done on evil level and should be justly revenged by My hand on them. Make no mistake; when time is correct, all this will end and they will perish as should be. None will respect them; none will help them, and none will remember them as men of honor. They will go into history as tyrants of the world, who died for dishonorable causes. This will give evil soul his revenge with Us in Heaven."

> If you are fighting terror with your own underhanded tactics, then this message from God applies also to you. We on Earth may not see how you are treating people around the world, but God sees everything. He will justify any wrongdoing His way. God is spelling out your punishment right here

• •

"What about suicide bombers? They believe they will go to Heaven if they bomb other people this way."

"I tell you to say of them, all who crush man get crushed from God. No one kills man without justice of God. All mankind is mine, I love all men. So to destroy a child of Mine; is to destroy My soul's love of them. Get thee in front of your maker and respect His way, until you realize who gave you life and who takes away life. You have no right ever, to take life of man I own. This is My child; all Earth is made up of children of Me."

"Can I put this part in the book?"

"Yes I will show you where everything I wish to be included should go.

"I tell you one more thing before you go. All in Heaven greatly wish Earth know how relish this Earth should be for each other. You should all know how to bring the best out of each other; instead of looking for the bad and making an issue of it. Then it will bring peace. Spend your time looking for the good in each other and of Me and not blaming each other for misfortune brought on by Satan. Do not blame God for bad happenings, and go back to your neighbors to apologize when you have harmed them. This is the way of heavenly souls, so if you want Us; you want this method of life."

• •

—God 8-12-06
"This I will say, your will has changed with Me, and for this all mankind will end correctly with Us. This was greatest gift you give this lands. I see your life with My will in it, giving courage to all who ask of your will for them also; **but always give answer to pray of Us, for only My answer will change their life. So of this way man can find God's way of their life also.**"

• •

"Here, God wanted to just give me some information."

"I wish to let you understand, that Our way will bring a review of what Our children do upon Earth. We will come in only few short months from Our daughter's success with this book; this is something not given others. But We have given you means of courage, for this day will frighten all upon Earth, even those with graced hearts will fear what they see above them; and will recognize Us among those with evil dwelling in them.

"I will say, "This is My Son, of whom all Earth has known justly; and now you see His voice is My voice. You will give Him My praise toward Him; because He has come with love of all mankind, for your salvation. You are indebted of He, who has your judgment of His hands.

"Then will say of them feared, 'Do I have love of all men?' If none answer Me; I leave your land forever more. But when they see evil souls at their sides; their hearts will melt of Me, and Earth will perish his evil more so. I give blessing over all Our mankind; then withdraw of Earth more.

"I tell you child your work is good way of giving more souls Our way, and many who die before this day, will grace your head praise, because of Us within you; they will live. Because you of Us, We will survive many.

"I know this statement will give many hardship when they read; but should stay in place. I see many with sources full that will doubt your ability, for they have not given Us freewill spirit. So they are going about life incorrectly; this will make them argue your writing. This is all of Us."

. . . .

"What is the next thing you want in this book?"

"Give Our plan with detailed instructions for all. Say We know you already have God's answers of life, this will review Our way of any who forget We are watching your progress thus created with man's knowledge. I, with My child (me), will give you Our reality course for actions taken of each day's Earth life.

"Never think We can't change what is written of Our way past history complies of any given; but I see Our world changes these, so I have also given many Our answers in recourse.

"Do what is said of Our Father and let go of what is acknowledged through churches, giving correct placement by scholars who have knowledge that is less than what We give Carol, here within these messages, given her thoughts with Us.

"No man is going to know what Our will for Our child with We, God, are about this way. She of Us will instruct all Earth; when I give her My blessing granting this woman child Our course of working of your Earth. So in this time grant her peace towards her mind and soul that all Earth will listen of her when God has told of His way."

• •

"I think you see Our way stronger this day, for you are thinking of good ways to explain this issue. I love this of your mind; that you spend Our time researching each set back for what occurred with your God.

"I will help adjust any areas you give too much effort of your own thought. Some will remain of you, for thoughts come through Me.

"I like this method you choose of historic knowledge increase. (Bible passages) All will understand My means of this holy book are intended more of teaching how I want Earth to respond to Me; than how to live away from Me. This be important for everyone to realize."

> God wants us all to realize that the Bible was written for us to know how to live with God everyday, as part of our life on Earth. Not to think of God as solely in Heaven and live our lives away from God as if He were an unapproachable being so far away.

> When you read the Old Testament, you see so many times how God speaks to people on Earth. He watches everything and adjusts everything to His will for them. In the New Testament, Jesus follows the will of God every moment, even unto His death. It shows how everyday Jesus prayed to know the will of the Father.

> These are the things in the Bible that God wanted us to realize. God is a living part of our lives. We are not to follow the teachings in the Bible as a guideline of how to live a good life. We are to follow the teaching in the Bible as a guideline of how to live with God everyday; doing His will for us, which He intended to give us on a daily bases. This plan teaches you God's method to do that very thing. The laws in the Bible are your guidelines to live a life intended by God. The stories however, are written to teach you this method to live in God's way.

• •

As you are most likely having doubts about what you are reading, I included this answer from God, regarding my doubt. In the beginning days of this new plan for my life, I was very frightened that I was not going to be able to do what God was telling me He wanted me to do. Remember that God wants us to accept this plan and to find others to share it with, so that all on Earth are living with God in this manner, since it is the only way to rid Earth of Satan. We, God's children, must make sure that Satan has no where on Earth to go.

"Give Me your days end; I will ease this heart ache. I tell you now this truth about God Us; We don't allow good souls for whom ask Our help to go unaided. You will get Our way first of all; then as We find your heart is entirely given Us, you will be allowed to give this message with love of Us, to all who are now holding you back from Our way. Give Us now forging cause of your will, for We have come with open heart and you must give."

. . . .

"Are evil spirits still going into a lot of people and staying with them?"

"All My children are holy until spirits within take them over for sin; but cast of them will make evil again angry towards God. This will bring evil war on your world, and foretell God's glory; for God has made you bring them to His end of they. I see your pain; it is Our God who bless your end, for they of faith will help God end evil for all time. This say the LORD God."

(This Poem Was Written By God)

When I call you, say, "I am coming LORD."
When I need you, run fast to My side;
When I praise you, tears well up for Me;
When I give you gifts, they are lonely be.

When you pray to Me, I give more to you;
When you answer Me, I tell all to you.
When you offer will to Me, I accept your life;
When you accept My will of you, I take away all strife.

Unknown Artist, Public Domain

"What images are okay for us to create of Jesus and Mary?"

"I want only His cross of resurrection shown; it never must give image, for Christ rose before Me."

"Mary?"

"Our Mother's will is sacred among Us. **Pray unto her through Our glory.** Give Our Lady graceful presence of this way show. Kneel of her form then ask her intervene with God toward your need with We Three LORD Host All. Never say toward Mother what should request of God; for God is all there be, that is powerful toward answer prayer of any who call Us."

—God

"To pray through Our glory means to come first before God in your prayer and then also give Mother Mary your thought. She wishes you know that Her answers also comes through Our will of both Her and you."

Benozzo Gozzoli 1420-1498 Public Domain

Mary has come to be with you,
Around your head she whispers;
Praise her name again today,
And she will smile in Heaven.

"Should there be statues of saints?"

"None, for they change God of us who call them. God wants no one should feel a saint is their way form. Hold only three images; Jesus of Nazareth, God with Son of hand toward world; then God of evil down of sword edge; and Mother of Earth, cast this devil form away, through might of God. All of these images justify God."

"God, can we keep images of Mary with Jesus, and also Joseph?"

"I allow only images that contain Holy family of Joseph with Mary and Child Jesus if they are given consideration of Joseph, as a man upon Earth, given charge over Christ Child while alive here of Earth. I do not allow intercession of My will through his name."

• •

God's comments during my morning prayers

Prayer for Intercession through the Blessed Mother

Our lovely lady ask Our LORD,
For gifts we need to see,
For in thy way is He who knows
Of all be in our say.

So this of you we ask today,
With hearts a full of love,
Mother of God be at our side,
When lessons need be learned;

For only God will give our way
When encouraged by your name.
Give her thanks.

"Jesus, will you tell me, when should I ask for you, and when the Father and when the Spirit?"

—Jesus—answers
"Give Me call, when you say, 'I am about my work, that Jesus has given me', show that We are with you in everything you experience with another. Call Holy Spirit, when you need guidance about your prayer with Father. Ask God all else."

"When should I ask for Angels?"

"They, I have given for everything. You can ask all times of them; I will be listening if they are around also. For all this is Heaven sent together; Father with us, Ghost and Me."

"Can we have images of Angels?"

—God—answer
"This I will allow because I see you require many forms around you to help you select good way of speaking heavenly of each other. I give Angels when I need your attention of My wish for you. They are here all the time of Our will for that purpose, and so because they represent My will, they are welcome images around Heaven and Earth."

. . . .

"How are those who don't know Jesus the son of God, going to get to Heaven?"

—Jesus—answer

"I have said the sick will heal in My presence, but none will see God unless carried to Him through My way.

"I leave you the Rosary of Our Mother for all salvation; this will make sick well, make lost find God, find hungry—feed, this will take souls through Purgatory to God, and guide soul's weak of heart."

"I judge of My father; if He gives permission when someone dies, then I give My will also for souls born of other courses, to enter the gates of Heaven. If God denies them, I say the same. God has My word on this issue towards their end. "Of the father no one has ignorance; all know God will bring them before him with judgment means strong. None have ever doubted they are not alone of His world; even the lowliest worms know God is their master being. For God does not give birth of such without giving sole means of life. It be given of them when life has given first birth; none have greater gift than knowing they are in His care always."

. . . .

"Tell me the proper way to look while praying?"

"Always give God first honor towards His soul by bending knees. Give proper garment; wear clothing that covers self pleasantly fit. No garment should address bosom, or chase away honor of Me. Cover yourself over these areas with gauze or you shall humiliate yourself in front of God."

"Should women wear something on their heads?"

"This will give humble look; though of Me, will only bring uncomfortable means given. I require your holy manners, this be enough."

. . . .

"Explain the creation of man?"

"I have given mankind all of My most honored gifts; you have just discovered Our LORD's holy way; so let Us say that none of Earth before you is given title with man in it. Animals were made of this Earth long before mankind is created;

not one animal has changed of man. So when this proof is shown, no Angel of God has come of it."

"Then You did consider what scientists on Earth are calling the evolution of man, as animals?"

"Yes, they are not what God created for company to Him. Man was given only that with Earth stride of man. All else has none of God's form within its being. So strong of case; but weak knowledge towards God has given you this scenario.

"God knows why these of Earth have given this say; Our LORD God will wipe out mankind when none know His way. So say of them, you have demand for they to put this straight for He. Give only His thoughts of this for we have heart worth love; no more life will see love for God but mankind. Man is of God, animal is of Earth."

> God wants us to stop saying that man evolved from an Ape. This is and was an animal in the eyes of God. This animal had no soul and no Angel, and did not die and go to Heaven. Mankind started with Adam and Eve. Please make these changes in regard to the history of mankind. This is the word of the LORD.

"Do animals go to Heaven?"

"None are of Heaven, for God sees them separate of mankind; they die, they don't have souls. They have peace when born. Knowledge of God is of mankind only. (Attaining God's will and also going to Heaven.) This is God's law for Earth."

· ·

"Are the spirit and soul separate?"

"The spirit is not soul, as you think, this is correct. But soul gives Us to you and provides you living of Us, while spirit gives living will power of your body so that when your body is whole united; all three, work together to give strength.

"Body alone is material source of life. Spirit alone gives challenge of heart, over Earth being, good answer of self. (Conscience, Mind, freewill)

"Soul alone, gives Us, with Our will for you while on Earth. (God within you, this gives life. Think of soul as your direct phone line to God or your God DNA.)

"Spirit lives only of the body on Earth; (Spirit stays with the body until judgment day.) Soul lives on eternally; (When you die, your soul goes to God and Jesus for judgment.) Body decays of Earth burial, thus is all."

> From this you can see why it is important to go to God for His will. If you don't access your soul's ability through God, you are left with the ability of spirit alone. Spirit can be influenced by Satan; Soul cannot. Soul is God within, and Satan cannot influence God.

"How is it then, that people see spirits?"

"People see spirits because these have no place on Earth to go when life ends of body. They sometimes walk around, wandering, until asked of Us to settle over their grave and wait of Us to call them from Earth. Some come in contact with evil souls who use them for fearing mankind; or giving wrong information to those who call upon spirits of dead bodies for knowledge, but none of heavenly being gives this." (None, whose souls are in Heaven, will be the spirits walking the Earth. These spirits are protected by God.)

"It is best for none with will of this kind, to come forth for other's means, to ask questions regarding their means of Earth. Mankind should be only willing God for all answers upon Earth.

"Spirits remain of the gravesite along with their body; this is of Our will for them. If bodies get moved, then those spirits forget their place of Earth, and challenge those around for means of their belonging place. This reason gives any who dig into a grave, after burial when body has passed, many unrewarding moments of doubt, regarding Our will for them. They have disturbed Our plan of Earth for self-involvement thus given and will suffer what happens to them when the spirit finds comfort within them, until otherwise given Our answer as to where they should go. Care should be taken not to disturb these sites further. For many who try this, will have many horrible ends; do to multiple being within them.

"When Earth is done, on the last day, I will open the graves and allow the spirits to rise to Heaven or be put to hell to suffer eternally. Only the spirit will come of Me, no bodies will be brought of Me. Bodies remain as evil source does, and will burn upon destruction of Earth. Spirit is considered pure, when it has come onto My will and I allow all who remain pure with good thoughts of Me, to rise to be with Me as Earth perishes when I decide its fate."

"If Satan used a spirit for evil, will you still consider it pure at the end of the Earth?"

"I say this, when evil is done of one with Me, I bless this soul so that this spirit will not be raised again with it. This soul becomes part with those around Us, never to have its spirit returned. This is not known of man because it is very evil to use these souls this way. "Satan has many times hurt Our people for this reason. They should know God forbids them call spirits thus, because doing so allows evil penetration into their forms to give wrong reward of you. These of your Earth relatives and friends lose Our call of these spirits once used by evil. Be aware that only pure of will come unto My home, none with evil dwell in Heaven.

"To make this clear, for any who wonder of good spirits among them; God does not allow good of will spirits for this reason. Good of will spirits remain separated from mankind until Earth ends."

"What you are saying is that any spirit seen on Earth has been used by Satan to confuse those who see them"

"This is correct, and should be stopped by humans who pursue this type of career. They are doing those spirits an injustice by forbidding them of Us.

"I say one thing more of this; I will bless only those who do My will of Earth. Those who torment good spirits with haunting homes, for the sake of inquiry will suffer My end of they. Those who ask of these spirits will cause Me to give many of them rewards done with evil source ahead." (An end with Satan)

The bottom line here is this: when you need answers, go to God alone for them. Don't ask your dead relatives or dead friends for help. Don't ask saints (who are dead) to help. Never ask anyone to contact someone's spirit. When you do this, you are giving Satan a call to go into those spirits for his evil purposes, and when that happens, God will not take those spirits to Heaven at the end of the world.

I will tell you this much: God will protect the spirits of the good, so the spirit you get may be whatever Satan has used to deceive you. Keep in mind that I told you there is a Purgatory. Not all souls go directly to Heaven or hell. So you do not know how your friends and family were judged at their death, so do not call their spirits, for fear you will give God reason not to bring that spirit up at the end of the world.

Don't pray to a saint to intervene with God; do not ask their spirit to come to you. *Simply ask them to pray for you.*

—God—continued

"They can also say they want My help through prayer from a saint on Earth. All who live a life with God in their heart for My will of them done are saintly with Me." So ask people you know on Earth to pray for you."

Unless you are praying to The Blessed Mother, you are not supposed to ask saints to intervene with God for your favor and never expect that your answer to your prayer is coming through them, because God is the only one who answers prayers.

Never take that away from God by saying "Saint . . . . answered my prayer." This is an insult to God. Remember that while those people were on Earth, they all knew that the miracles attributed to them were not by them, but by God. That is the reason they are saints, because all of them knew who the power was behind the miracle. They all loved God very deeply and did the will of God, not their own will. These people prayed for God's will and then knowing His will they were given jobs to do for God that allowed God to use them to create His miracles on Earth. On their own, they were simply men and women the same as you and I. Instead of praying to them, you should be imitating their behavior. To intervene means to interfere in the will of God. I don't think any of the saints want you to ask them to do that.

When St. Paul talked about saints in his letters to the churches, he was referring to all of mankind that lived in the will of God. He meant you and me who know God is all there is. He never said pray to a saint for intervention with God; he said, ask saints to pray for you, meaning ask those who live in God's grace to pray for you. You should be praying for each other, and then you become saintly with God.

God uses those who ask His will to bring those who have not asked His will closer to Him, so that all mankind understands His power and love over their lives. Each miracle is a reminder for you that God wants you to come closer to Him. Then He will give you everything you need and every blessing He has been waiting to give you. God has so many gifts waiting for those who just simply ask.

Asking means giving up your freewill, and asking for God's will for you. This way of asking gets you everything Heaven has to offer you. Asking in a selfish way, by not offering anything first to your Creator, gets you very little. God holds back His blessings for those who don't hold back their love of Him. The rest just get enough to survive. They get an Angel to help them who has to work overtime to keep them from totally falling into Satan's hands, and they get blessings for their good deeds and prayers. But when we come to God totally, the good of all Heaven is open to us.

• •

"If someone is not baptized in water and spirit, how will they get images from you?"

"I will allow all to image My will for them no matter which religion or rites they have received, for now is a new beginning of man through Our will. All will come of My will for them."

• •

"Will anyone else hear you like I hear you?"

"None will know Our word for you have been selected of your mercy of others to bring Our words for them. They will be allowed visions of their purpose for Our will.

"I say one thing of this: When any of My children ask of My blessing through will for them, they will receive all I have of them. None will be denied, for all are equal of Us on high.

"Give this for they must know all is about My will only. Your name of Us is always given with blessings attached, for We know how intensely you give Our word."

• •

—Carol
"Father, are the stories of the Old Testament only stories to teach lessons or are they true?"

—God

"These, My child are current with Us. For any who know God, know how truth will always give."

—Carol

"So then David killed the giant with a stone?"

—God

"This is correct version."

—Carol

"And these three men, Shadrach, Meshach and Abed-nego were sent into a fire?"

—God

"They live of Us now and can say this happened."

—Carol

"Noah and the ark?"

—God

"Yes I have given account testify"

—Carol

"All accounts in the Bible, in the Old Testament really happened?"

—God

"This will be the truth, for only through Us can true evidence be drawn of those born prior to this time. I give writings of this to show future man the power involved with believing Our words."

—Carol

"Were any of the stories of the Old Testament considers parables?"

—God

"None were untrue tales for hide truth. Only done of Jesus, for protect until His time correctly cast His end. All that know Me through Jesus, know Our way through His answers. He gave correct way of man to approach God Almighty. All need recognize LORD Jesus through His teachings. Those who do not know Him, do not know Me."

—Carol

"How should I tell people to ask for healing or favors from you, through me?"

—God

"Say, 'I am only God's humble servant, if you require God for service to you; ask only for Jesus Christ, to give blessings of your souls force in nature. This will bring His presence.'"

Please, never ask me to heal you; I have no ability on my own. To honor God; if you see me, ask only for Jesus Christ.
"I need the mercy of Jesus Christ to heal me."
"I need the love of Jesus Christ to help me know the will of God."
"I need the strength of Jesus Christ to give me courage against evil spirits around me.

I will say the prayers, given to me by God that will bring Jesus to both of us, for what you need. Also, if you write to me, please start your letter by asking for Jesus in this same manner, and I will pray to God before I read your letter, to ask Jesus to come and be with both of us as I answer your letter.

After you receive help from Jesus, say this prayer for the three days following. This was given to me, from Our Blessed Mother, as a prayer of thanksgiving.

"Jesus Christ, child of God, You have graced me with Your presence and because of Your divine mercy and love; You have brought life's strength back to me. For this and for all Your suffering on the cross, in my honor, I thank Your Divine Soul."

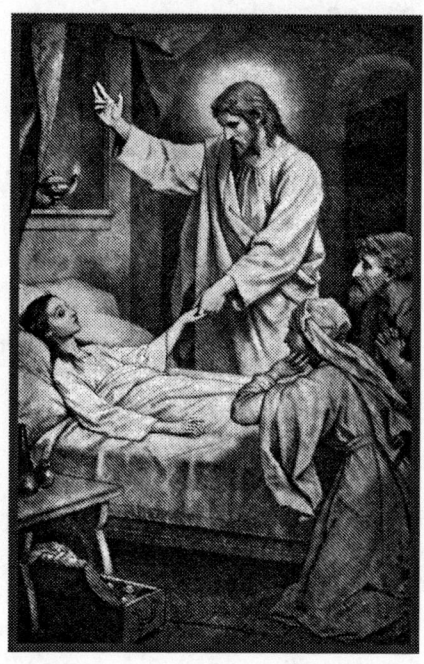

Unknown Artist, Public Domain

"The Story of the Tortured Stars."

In fall of 1998, my husband and I were driving to my mom's house, and while he drove, I read a book aloud. In the book, it said that you should pick a symbol for your path in life.

The sun had already set, and it was beginning to get darker, so I wanted to take a minute to look out at the beautiful fall colors on the Michigan trees. When I finished the chapter and put the book down, I turned to my husband and said, "What do you think I should pick?"

Immediately after saying that, I turned to the side window for a look around, and noticed that the window was completely filled with a bright, full moon. I took that as an indication of what my life path sign should be.

I normally slept during the 45 minute drive home, but this time, I put a tape of Spanish Guitar music into the tape player and closed my eyes to meditate.

I asked God, "What is my moon path?" I then received a vision of a blue star in the center of a white piece of paper. Near the top left of the star, it said, **"Start the process . . ."** I was surprised to get it, as well as confused. It was signed at the bottom right, **"God."** So I asked God, "What do you want me to do with that star?" I was then shown a picture of the moon shining along the pathway that lead to an old friend's door. Well of course I didn't want to believe that God wanted me to take him the star. I hadn't seen this man in over seven months, and felt foolish about showing up at his door with a picture of a star that said, 'Start the process . . . God.'

So the next day, on my way home from work, I decided to ask for a sign. I had been told quite a few times in the previous weeks to watch for signs; and to tell you the truth, I had never put much faith in that before. However, that day I needed a sign or I wasn't going to paint a star and bring it to someone. So being very clever . . . I thought . . . I said to God, "Okay God, if you want me to do this, show me a star."

Now, I knew that there were no Chrysler buildings along this street, and I didn't remember seeing a star on anything on my way home before. So I figured this would be a true sign, if God found a star to show me.

Well, within 30 seconds, a black car pulled in front of me,
and my eyes were drawn to the license plate.
There were no numbers on it.
It was black with white writing, and read:

ALL STAR

Of course I was pretty shocked. I just looked up to Heaven and said, "Okay God, I'll do it!" I painted it (badly) and took it to the person God wanted it to go to. "Yes, it was very uncomfortable to show up with a terrible cold, in the rain, with a painted message from God, but my old friend made me a hot drink to soothe my throat, and we talked for hours, neither one of us knowing why God sent him that message until weeks later. The message was God's way to help him with work he was doing.

The day after Christmas that same year, I asked God again for some financial help. His reply came in the form of more visions, eleven in all, and given in less than one hour. I was sketching like crazy, so as not to forget any of them. These were more stars that God wanted to get to people.

I promised God I would get the stars to people He chose, one way or another. I just figured that God would direct people to the stars, if that was his will. I worked for years to make them look the way they looked in my mind. I never gave up, no matter how many setbacks I had, and there were plenty of them that would frustrate even the most patient person.

My mom, sisters and my nephews supported my efforts by giving me first, a small gold pendant that I wear all the time. The pendant has an Angel on one side, and a star with a tear drop (my logo for the Tortured Stars) on the other. Next I received a blue Crystal star to hang in front of a window, or wear around my neck. They then found a little copper star with a tear drop, a blue stone star, and an Angel wind chime that I have hanging in my bedroom. So you see, God keeps directing them to things that will keep me focused, and so for my birthday or Christmas they are surprised to find these for me, and I am delighted to get them. My husband has been a rock, and just lets me do whatever I have to do in order to fulfill my promise to God. Thank God for this man's patience with me. I also have a few other friends who verbally supported my efforts, and believe me, all of it was appreciated.

I am sharing this story with you to let you know that the will of God is not always something you can do instantly. So never give up when you know God is counting on your efforts. You may find a lot of people won't believe why you're doing these things, but don't let that stop you, either. Do the will of God with strong conviction, and soon people will start giving you the benefit of the doubt, which is the starting place of truth. Before long, they will start to ask how they can find out God's will for them.

After I received the Angel message on April 5, 2006, I realized that the images God gave me many years ago were to be presented at this time. So as you see, everything is done when God wants it done.

God did not name these 'Tortured Stars', I did. They were named for the amount of torture they gave me and the amount of torture I gave them through the process. I eventually got them to look close to the images God gave me, so now; they are in the hands of an artist and God.

These images will be available on products, hopefully in the first few months of '2008'. We are doing our best to keep these products as inexpensive as possible because they are artistic messages from God.

Letter to Friends and Family

—Carol

Many of the people, who will read this book and/or hear about it, have known me for years. To those people, I wish to say I appreciate and cherish the part you played in my life. God has asked me not to give much information about my past because it is just that: The past. Our LORD has changed me and the course of my life to His will for me, because I asked for His will.

I have asked God to give many blessings to all of you who protect my life as if it were your own. God has asked me to do work for Him with people who need to trust me to give them the word of God, to help them find God in their own lives. I will need the love and support of all who hold my new life's work in their hands and protect my privacy.

Many people, who want to hurt me because of the work of Satan to stop me, will approach you to ask you to give them information about me. This is not what the will of God is for you, so please be careful not to speak of my life prior to today. Instead, talk about this plan with graced gratitude toward God, who has given us all a renewed hope for our lives and this Earth, and has come to save us from all evil that tormented and hurt us for centuries.

You all have my love, and if it is God's will, while I travel around the world for Him, we will see each other for a new cause of friendship between us.

I also ask you to keep in mind that I have been working hard to be as humble and worthy of God's grace as I can. (I am smiling, because God has been teaching me this the hard way.) So give me no reasons to be prideful. Say neither things that would bring harm to me nor things that would bring pride to me. I am beginning to sound like St Paul here, so I am ending this page.

—God

"I add this: should evil come upon My child in her work, I will be there for her aid. All who know her of yesterday are her brothers and sisters through Me. This, My family is important; protect her, your sister as I protect her.

—God—continued

I have answered her praise of you and will bless they who know her, many times over, for giving My will first priority when approached by evil means to destroy her reputation of Earth.

"My blessing on your heads, begins with the moment of publication due this novel of main event, given here within and continues stronger when approached of evil be."

I thank you all.
Your sister in God and friend,
Carol (mustard seed)
Love each other.

Sandro Botticelli 1445-1510 Public Domain

I give you more, less none will see
We have arrived to thee,
To give our world more help of late,
For God wish company.

End Note

As an end note,
I just want to say that when you pray to God,
don't do all the talking,
sit quietly and listen.
You might be surprised what you hear.

I hope you hear Angels, too.

God, bless all of us. Amen.

—Carol
"What do You think God? Did I do a good job for You?" *(I was just thinking this question to myself, not really expecting an answer. Sort of a rhetorical question!)*

—God
"This I am proud; for this of God has been given." *(I was surprised when God answered me and it made me smile to know He was listening.)*

—Carol
"Is that You, God?" *(So I looked up at my Father in Heaven and could not wipe the broad smile off my face as I teased Him back.)*

—God
"This, I Am." *(I felt His warm love come over me, as He answered me.)*

—Final Message from God

This message is a little confusing because God keeps changing from one spirit to another. So basically this message is from God the Father; God the Son, Jesus Christ; and God the Holy Spirit.

"This problem, which We have come together to amend for His Earth is Our most important chore. Nothing based of Earth has as much known charm, for evil against souls than he (Satan) which God is now forcing back away towards his (Satan) end.

"Let it be perfectly clear of all who struggle in believing these words within, that it is Our God Almighty's grace alone that is giving you His command; for now is your time of repentance. This plan has His holy structure, so that ye with Earth are given His way for saving God's name among men who trust God to give eternal life, when this world of yours does no more exist.

"No further repentance, of He (God) who lives above, will please His most Holy Son, Jesus Christ, than seeing peoples and nations give Almighty God's grace/will first effort every day. Should none understand the significance, of this process, Our Carol can give all Our instruction through grace from His Almighty LORD.

"No effort of God towards His children is mislead.

"I am His way. (Holy Spirit speaking of God the Father) My end is without error. I do not curse of this evil one, for he (Satan) is Mine. I am without sin of heart, for evil only exists for Earth. This planet is My wills. My source above will guide Me of His way, (Holy Spirit speaking of God the Father) should I need of this."

—Carol—question
"May I ask who is speaking through the Holy Spirit?"

—God
"This be Our God's source be."

—Carol—question
"So then, You are the Holy spirit of God?"

—God
"My daughter child, My soul of souls, My work of love; please Me of this . . . for your heart knows I am; yet this is asked of those who doubt us together."

> I just want you to know that Our Heavenly Father speaks of all His children with this same love as He has spoken to me in this answer. It is thrilling to hear God, our creator, tell you . . . that you have pleased Him.

—Carol—question
"What things should I say to Your souls? Is there something in the Bible that I should say?"

—God
"This I say to you, only say of what is present. The end will be, before Earth grows."

—Carol—question
"What does that mean?"

—God
"This means I have no further plans regarding expanding Earth. What I have given will remain said of Me. No god of this life has give more love for they. Only that . . . I of Me . . . that has this source of love all."

—Carol—question
"Is there anything else that needs to be put into this book?"

—God
"Only this, now your hearts live in fear and darkness; belonging instead, with painful ends of he (Satan) who takes soul's minds away towards he (Satan). But have some help with Us of God's will, so that Earth's strife with hell's end, will no more cause his (Satan) pressures against Me of LORD God.

"Many will come this way/time; because they will see his (Satan) darkened heart has taken safety of life from them. They will judge their own action, with his evil ways. They can enter into God's Kingdom, if following His Holy way, through doing work towards giving others Our God's plan, so that all has need fulfilled.

"Be ever so kind of they who look away from you through this effort; for God wants all of they who participate of His plan, for rid evil's name of Earth; to give spirit with this, on his or her own efforts, because there will be given of God's way."

> God wants all of us to come to Him on our own, not to try to force anyone into doing this plan, but He wants you to simply present it to them, the way God is presenting it to you. God does not tell anyone to do His will; He waits for you to come to Him freely. This plan is to show Satan that *we choose God*, and that *we are not being forced to choose God*. Our God is all love and our way through God . . . is all love.

—God

"No one can enter Gates from Heaven on force of will from other power (Satan). So careful, of all who ask for power that help (People, who have evil within them). For only God has answer of this. Be smart in choices, when offered his help that knows of better way. (People who are telling you that this plan will not work.) For he (Satan) knows little, when God is around you."

> This paragraph is referring to Satan, who will be trying to tell you he is helping you, through people who do not have your best interest at heart. But do not believe any source for help, without prayers to God in advance to send Satan on his way. Always go to God first, everyday and follow what God wants you to do. If you are not sure about help offered to you from anyone else, you can contact me and I will ask God for you. But always think about answers you get from anyone. If you are being told to do anything against the will of God, then your source is not correct.

—**God**
"Now give this to all of Earth

"Bow thy head in Our LORD God's presence . . . as I with He (Holy Spirit
and God) . . . give of His grace over your minds . . . so that he (all of us) **with
God . . . will know when God has forgiven all.**

**"Praise God with everything you do. Only of this . . .
can Heaven grace of you, all that is of They.
Amen."**

Be sure to bow your head for this blessing from God. He knows you
are reading His plan, and has promised to Grace everyone who reads
this book with the knowledge to understand its importance.

Acknowledgments

Reserved for e-book	**Steven Barker** © 2007 Book Cover
Luca Giordano—Fa Presto Neopolitan 1632-1705 Public Domain Image	**Steven Barker** © 2007 Angel
Giotto di Bondone 1276-1337 Public Domain Image	**Jan Van Eyck** 1385-1441 Public Domain Image
Pietro di Cristoforo 1450-1523 Public Domain Image	**Michelangelo Buonanoti** 1475-1564 Public Domain Image
Lorenzo Ghiberti 1378-1455 Public Domain Image	**Leonardo da Vinci** 1451-1519 Public Domain Image
Gustave Dore 1833-1883 Public Domain Image	**Virchi d Pietro Perugino** 1450-1523 Public Domain Image
Raffaello Sanzio 1483-1520 Public Domain Image	**The Bellman** 2004 Public Domain Image
William Adophe 1825-1905 Public Domain Image	**Gerard Van Honthorst** 1590-1656 Public Domain Image
Shonda ReneaL © 2005 *http://www.reneal.com*	**Benozzo Gozzoli** —Florentine 1420-1498 Public Domain Image
Guido Remi 1575-1642 Public Domain Image	**Sandro Botticelli** 1445-1510 Public Domain Image

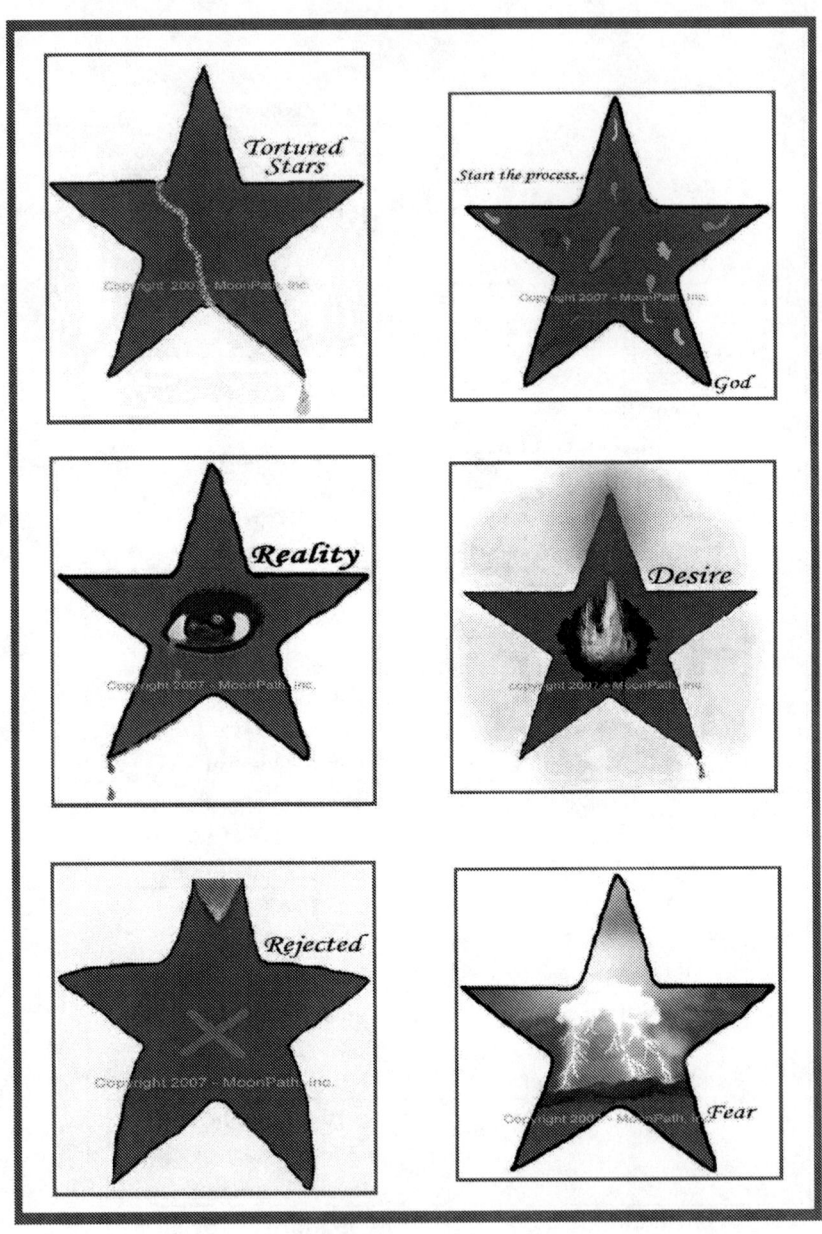

Carol Aubuchon © 2007

These are 11 of the 12 'Tortured Stars.' Of course, by the looks of them, you can tell these are the ones I did, and not the ones being worked on by Steven Barker. I didn't want to tell you the story, and not show you what the stars actually are. I am looking forward to presenting these to you after so many years. Now you know why I call them tortured.

Heartbreak

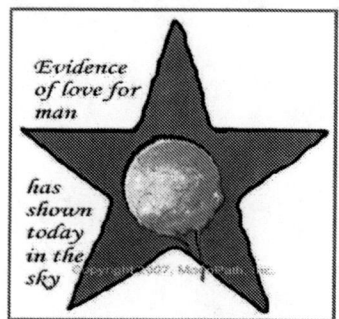

Evidence
of love for
man

has
shown
today
in the
sky

Escape

Empty

Sanctuary

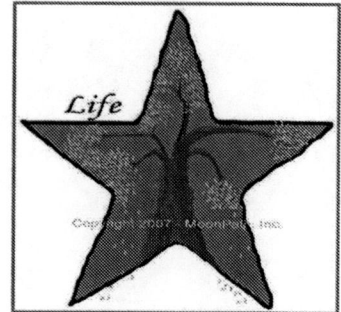

Life

CPSIA information can be obtained at www.ICGtesting.com
Printed in the USA
239508LV00011B/15/A